WILLIAMS
SONOMA
CALIFORNIA

Newlywed Cookbook

⚭

PHOTOGRAPHY BY JOHN KERNICK

weldon**owen**

Contents

delicious simplicity
Just a few seasonal ingredients, elegantly paired, result in satisfying dishes like this Spaghettini with Cauliflower Pesto (recipe page 144).

Love & Food: Cooking Together

When you tie the knot, the two of you will probably already have some sense of your way around a kitchen. Most couples getting married today have already mastered at least one favorite recipe, navigated the stalls of a farmers' market, or shared in the preparation of a meal. Most of you have set up house with roommates, on your own, or as a couple and bring some history of food traditions and opinions with you—in addition to a favorite banged-up pot, beloved knife, or can't-do-without stand mixer.

What makes the newlywed kitchen unique is the way you experience it together and what that says about you as a couple. In this room that smells of fresh-baked scones and bacon or soy sauce and kimchi, you will work side by side. Even if one of you is the cook and the other the bottle washer, here you will stir, whisk, laugh, wrap, rinse, toast, roast, cork-pop, argue, pour, cheer, scrub, buff, boil, and baste—together cooking up memories you'll savor for a lifetime.

This book aims to help today's couples inhabit their kitchen with love. Everyone needs a little advice from time to time, including tips on organizing a kitchen that works for two, stocking a pantry and refrigerator, collecting cookware and tableware, and ably creating cozy breakfasts, workday meals, gatherings with friends, and new holiday traditions. The recipes are infused with global flavors, seasonal ingredients, some retro nostalgia, and lots of flexibility—most can be customized to suit your particular tastes.

The hope is that this book will inspire collaboration. Think of it as date night in the kitchen, where you have a chance to create something with two pairs of hands while sharing a glass of wine and a quiet moment. With this approach, your time spent preparing homemade food can become some of the most memorable moments you spend together.

A Fresh Philosophy

The first rule of the modern kitchen, and the foundation of the recipes in this book, is to cook with the seasons. Yes, we live in a time where food is flown around the globe so we have the possibility of asparagus in winter and pomegranates in summer, but thanks to the farmers' market revolution of the past few decades, we know that seasonal foods taste best and that buying from local farmers benefits the environment and makes economic sense. Plus, the food is really good for you.

SUPERFOODS: COOKING FOR A LONG LIFE

Diet trends come and go, but eating fresh, seasonal foods in a rainbow of colors is always good policy. In recent years, certain foods have been singled out for high nutrient content, antioxidant and anti-inflammatory properties, boosting metabolism, and fighting health conditions from heart disease to cancer. Lists may vary, but these are some of the most common—and most delicious—superfoods to incorporate into your meals for a long, healthy life together.

ALLIUMS garlic, leeks, onions, shallots

BERRIES blackberries, blueberries, cranberries

FATTY FISH sustainably harvested salmon and sardines, fresh or canned

FERMENTED FOODS miso, sauerkraut, yogurt

NUTS & SEEDS almonds, flaxseeds, hazelnuts, sesame seeds, walnuts

SPICES black pepper, cayenne, ginger, turmeric

VEGETABLES avocados, beets, cruciferous vegetables (broccoli, brussels sprouts, kale, cabbage, collards), leafy greens (chard, spinach), sweet potatoes

OTHER dark chocolate, green tea, seaweed (wakame, kelp, nori)

a kitchen garden

Nothing tastes better than vegetables and fruits that you've grown yourself—and you don't need a large yard to cultivate with success. Try growing herbs and container-friendly produce, such as lettuce and strawberries, on a deck, patio, or balcony. Vessels have come a long way beyond the terra-cotta pot: Options include wall-mounted vertical planters, ladder-like vertical growing systems, portable elevated beds, and vintage tubs and basins on stands. Choose an area that gets at least four hours of full sunlight, preferably near a wall that holds the heat. You can also grow mixed greens inside in pots on a sunny shelf or window box. Use good-quality potting soil and containers with drainage holes or planting bags to collect water.

heirloom variety

**Use produce in a range of colors
and flavors and each dish you
prepare becomes a special one.**

Setting Up a Kitchen for Two

Whether you've literally just walked over a new threshold or been living together for a while, now is the perfect time to create a kitchen that is comfortable and efficient for both of you—especially if you're not sure where to put your wedding gifts.

Start by decluttering worn-out cookware and redundant or no longer needed tools. Then, together, find a location for the items you want to keep.

To determine where and how to store your kitchen accoutrements, it might help to think of the kitchen as having three work areas, with the goal of streamlining what it takes to get tasks done in each:

PREP refrigerator, sink, adjacent counter space, and pantry

COOKING stove, oven, and adjacent counter space

CLEANUP sink, dishwasher, and drying area

Not sure where to begin? Mock-cook a recipe with one of you in the prep area and the other in the cooking area. Practice reaching for items you need for each area: Where are the knives and cutting boards? Are the colanders near the sink? Can you put a pan on the stove, grab a wooden spoon, and reach for the salt without bumping into each other? Are the potholders within grabbing distance of the stove and the oven? Where's a handy place to hang and store kitchen towels?

If there is a baker in the house, consider choosing a section of the counter dedicated to baking, and put the flour and sugar canisters there with the stand or handheld mixer, cake and tart pans, cooling racks, and other baking items in nearby storage space. If there is space, set up a breakfast station with coffee and tea canisters, mugs, espresso machine, milk frother, cereal bowls, spoons, and juice glasses, because making breakfast without stepping on each other's toes is a nice way to start the day. Arrange things artfully, but don't worry about perfection; it's okay for a lived-in kitchen to have a lived-in look.

No kitchen is perfect at all times, just as no marriage is. The best advice? Divide and collaborate (rather than divide and conquer) and work as a team, enjoying the camaraderie and communicating all the while. With your four hands, the goal of producing a great meal is made easier in your well-laid-out kitchen.

Cooking for Two: Making It Special

If you spend a lifetime making the most of each moment together, then every minute will be like one from your honeymoon—not a bad way to live. Eating and cooking together can be among the most intimate moments you share. The key is to keep it fresh: Try recipes you've never made, dine in places you've never considered—don't just plunk down in front of the TV or computer. Approach your meals thoughtfully and with style because when it comes to setting the mood, presentation counts almost as much as the food.

BREAKFAST IN BED Especially when you're a newlywed, any day is a good day to share breakfast in bed. Think of it as a mini-honeymoon, and trade off who cooks. Bring out all those special wedding gifts: the French press or china teapot, linens you reserve for holidays, good silver, a crystal vase with a fresh flower. Then cuddle up together over breakfast.

INDOOR PICNIC Sunshine and cool grass aren't the only requirements for a top-notch picnic. When the weather turns cold and gray, take your picnic indoors. Start your meal with soup in chunky mugs or ceramic bowls. Spread a blanket on the living room floor (next to the fireplace if you have one) and eat off picnicware, then finish with brownie s'mores (page 233) or use long skewers to toast marshmallows in the fire.

CELEBRATION FRIDAY Celebrate the end of the week with sparkling wine or cocktails (pages 86–87) and simple appetizers, such as spiced nuts (page 75) or warm olives (page 74). Use your wedding crystal, or even better, the flutes you toasted with on the day of your ceremony, then take some time to recall a humorous time you shared or to revisit the characteristics you appreciate in each another.

DREAM DESTINATION Cook a recipe from a dream vacation spot, add some of the native landscape to your table decor, and put some destination music on your playlist. Whether it's Korean-style short ribs (page 157) or classic French crepes (page 46), a culinary journey takes armchair travel to a delectable new level (and may put some of your lesser-used kitchen wedding registry items to good use).

SPA STAYCATION Make smoothies or fill a bar shaker with your favorite cocktail, take a few glasses from the cabinet, and slip into a bath together.

friendly competition
Challenge each other to make a dish you've never made before or to use a piece of equipment you've never tried. For pastry lovers, yeast doughnuts (page 31) are a great way to put the deep-fry thermometer to work. Or try the immersion blender for a puréed soup. Get out the mandoline and shave cucumber to go with rice noodles (page 107). Blend up a béarnaise sauce (page 248). Fire up the kitchen torch and brûlée to perfection (page 210).

express your love
Prepare a special dessert
for your sweetheart like this
delicious Raspberry-Lemon
Tart (recipe page 243) as a
declaration of your sentiments.

savor every moment

The kitchen can be a shared haven—a special place to unwind, to reconnect, and relate the stories of your day. Enjoy it with a glass of good wine, your favorite music, and your best friend beside you.

Cooking for a Crowd

Cherishing moments with just the two of you is always a good thing, but entertaining as a couple is also a ton of fun. It's creative, generous, personal, and memorable. You can make it a sit-down dinner in the dining room, an appetizers party in the living room, a quick Sunday brunch on the deck, or an all-day open house. Whatever the gathering, success depends on just one thing: everyone feeling relaxed and happy—especially the hosts.

CHECKLIST FOR A GREAT PARTY

CHOOSE A DATE Saturday nights aren't the only time to have a party. A weeknight spaghetti feed is a great way to get together with friends, and a long, relaxed Sunday lunch commonly works better than a rager the night before.

DECIDE ON THE GUEST LIST Close friends? All couples? Coworkers? A new neighbor? The guest list determines the style of the party. Only close friends means a small and intimate affair. A bigger group, where guests move around and mingle, is best for a more casual gathering, such as a cocktail party or barbecue.

MANAGE THE MENU Choose a variety of colors, textures, and serving temperatures in your dishes so they taste and look beautiful together. Choose a recipe that you've made at least once before, and select dishes that have staggered cooking times with different cooking methods (oven, microwave, and stove top) to make life easier.

SHOP, COOK, PREP Divvy up tasks between the two of you, make lists, and assign jobs. Make a shopping list, noting anything that needs to be purchased the day of the party, such as ice. Double-check that you have the cookware and tools you need. Set the table a day in advance. Chop, bag, and chill vegetables. Make ahead whatever you can, such as dips, salad dressings, and dessert.

THINK DRINKS Consider wine and beer choices based on your menu. Set up your home bar (see left). Buy bottles of fizzy water for nondrinkers. Make sure you have enough glasses, ice, and cocktail napkins. Offer coffee and tea after dinner.

THINK APPETIZERS Be sure to offer something to go with the cocktails, even just pita chips and dip (page 74). Guests should have something in their hands—a beverage and a small bite—almost as soon as they walk through the door.

DON'T FORGET Flowers, lighting, music, napkins, and ice; hand towels and soap in the bathroom. And, remember, a party is fun for the guests if it's fun for the hosts, so relax and enjoy the party, and your friends and family will, too.

---

setting up a home bar

Almost as much creativity goes into cocktails these days as into cooking. Find a corner shelf, cabinet, or rolling cart for setting up your bartending station. Be sure to match your glassware to the type of drink. Garnishes can also be an important addition; have on hand martini olives, cocktail onions, and maraschino cherries, as well as a citrus stripper and plenty of limes, lemons, and oranges for zesting.

BOOZE Aperol or Lillet, bourbon and/or Scotch, brandy, Campari, gin, dark and light rum, tequila, dry and sweet vermouth, vodka.

MIXERS Tonic water, soda water, ginger ale, lemon-lime soda, and Coca-Cola.

TOOLS Cocktail shaker, strainer, mixing glass or pitcher, jigger, ice tongs, stirring spoon, corkscrew, bottle opener, citrus press, muddler, zester, ice bucket, water pitcher.

GLASSWARE Martini glasses or coupes for strained drinks, Old-Fashioned glasses for mixed drinks or straight pours, tall highball glasses for drinks made with carbonated water or mixers, cordial glasses for Amaro and digestives, brandy snifters, Champagne flutes, wineglasses for red and white wines, beer mugs or glasses.

Setting the Table

Whether you like to entertain, or to cook just for the two of you, a little bit of table setting know-how is a nice way to begin your married years.

THE TRADITIONAL TABLE

The classically appointed table begins with some knowledge of what is to be served and when. Arrange the napkin, flatware, and glasses around the plate in order of use. The napkin goes to the left of the plate, folded edge toward the diner, so it can be picked up and unfolded on the lap.

FLATWARE The forks go to the left of the napkin, dinner fork on the inside and salad fork on the outside (since in a formal meal, salad is served first). If there is a special course, such as one that might require an oyster or fish fork, the fork should be placed on the table in the order it will be used (first course to the farthest left). To the immediate right of the plate, place the main-course knife, blade facing in, so it can be picked up in the right hand and be ready to use, then the spoon. Above the plate, place the dessert fork, tines facing to the right, and the dessert spoon, bowl facing to the left.

GLASSWARE Glassware should be arranged in a diagonal line above the main-course knife, in order of use from closest to farthest. The water glass or goblet is closest to the plate since it is used throughout the meal, then the red wineglass, and finally the white wineglass because it is usually paired with the first course.

TABLEWARE If there is a bread plate, place it to the left of the forks and just above them, with the butter knife on the top edge of the plate, parallel to the edge of the table, blade pointing down.

THE INFORMAL TABLE

There are really no hard and fast rules of thumb when it comes to setting the table for an informal gathering. At each seat, place a plate, with a fork to its left and knife to its right, and a napkin either under the fork or folded and placed on the plate. For a family-style or buffet meal, stack plates and put flatware in jars or tall glasses or inside rolled-up napkins so guests can grab their own setting. Provide each guest with a water glass and a wineglass, stemmed or not (like simple tumblers). Provide a pitcher full of water or two. Serve wine in bottles or carafes. If you are serving beer, provide glasses for that as well, or bottles and a few openers to pass around. Arrange food on platters or in bowls. Bread can go in baskets, and cheese can go on boards. Don't forget serving utensils, such as large spoons, ladles, and salad tongs.

tablescaping

Linens, lighting, and flowers help establish the mood of any gathering. Traditional or formal settings used to call for a pressed linen tablecloth, but a simply appointed table can also achieve elegance. Atmospheric lighting is important: Candlesticks and votives with unscented candles add the intimacy of candlelight. For flowers, choose either one dramatic variety, such as peonies or roses, or an arrangement, keeping the height low enough so it doesn't block conversation or your view across the table.

Even a casual table, set with confidence, can have its own measure of insouciant style. For sit-down meals, adorn the table with fresh cuttings from the garden nestled into bell jars, or even a slender tree branch set down the middle. In the evenings, rely on the twinkling of votive candlelight or small clusters of chunky candles to set the mood.

dining alfresco

Take your meals outdoors and experience Mother Nature's best seasoning: fresh air.

Cooking & Eating Outdoors

Once you have everything squared away indoors, it's time to focus your attention outside. Whether you prepare food alfresco on a patio grill or a hibachi on a fire escape, nothing seasons food better than fresh air. Most couples who appreciate outdoor cooking know that nearly anything that can be cooked in the oven can also be accomplished on the grill: sturdy vegetables, stone fruits, pineapple, pizza, paella, polenta, tofu, even dessert. If you master flavorful glazes, marinades, and rubs that can be brushed onto proteins and vegetables, you can vary the menu endlessly. Learn how to adjust the heat on your grill; with the top closed, you can use it like an outdoor oven.

SETTING THE OUTDOOR TABLE

When it's just the two of you, cooking and dining outdoors can be a cozy way to spend the evening together. When friends are over, keep it casual by piling food from the grill onto platters for easy serving. Make evening meals special by looping string lights over the dining table, fastening a flickering candelabra to an adjacent tree branch, or arranging uplights (either solar or electric) in the nearby landscape. If you have room, set aside a few comfortable outdoor chairs (or even some plump throw cushions) to lounge on during cocktail hour. Like the kitchen in your indoor home, your cooking area will probably be the hub of your outdoor one, so make your outdoor living area within easy access of the grill and the table.

PACK A PICNIC

Staying at home is nice, but packing a basket or backpack for a portable meal outdoors can add some of the spice of life to the meals you share. Load your carryall with metal or melamine plates and jelly jars for glasses, all wrapped in linen dish towels so they don't rattle. Pour drinks into a thermos or large jar for easy transport. Prepare a bacon-Gruyère quiche (page 56) and cookies (pages 237–239) for dessert, and head to the park, beach, mountains, or your own backyard. Spread out some of the dish towels as little tablecloths (saving two for napkins) and take in a casual meal away from the distractions of your home environment.

All About Wine

Opening a bottle and pouring a glass of wine is a happy ritual indeed. The best way to learn about wine is to taste it. Establish a relationship with a wine merchant you trust, then collect varietals that interest you and try them with different foods. Store extra bottles away from light and heat in an area that has an even temperature, below 70°F (21°C) if possible. Place bottles on their sides or upside down to keep their corks moist; dry corks allow air into the bottle, which oxidizes the wine. Serve white wine in smaller glasses with U-shaped cups, red wine in broader and rounder glasses. The bowls of wineglasses are designed to enhance the aromatic experience of each varietal.

WINE & FOOD PRIMER

CHAMPAGNE/SPARKLING WINES Bubbly always feels like a celebration, so always have a bottle at the ready to make any moment a special one. Champagne (from a denominated region in France), Prosecco, Cava, and other dry sparkling wines from Italy, Spain, California, and elsewhere are wonderful with oysters, salty appetizers, even light risotto and fish dishes.

CRISP WHITES Keep a chilled bottle on hand for daily drinking and for sipping with global foods and spicy dishes. Sauvignon Blanc, Pinot Grigio, Sancerre, and Grüner Veltliner are excellent choices.

RICH WHITES Chardonnay is always popular with appetizers and for drinking with chicken or buttery, creamy dishes.

ROSÉS Blush wines offer a crisp flavor and fruity character perhaps best suited to sipping on a summer evening and for serving with alfresco lunches, spicy dishes, and cured meats.

LIGHT REDS Beaujolais and Pinot Noir are wonderful for both sipping and for serving with vegetarian dishes, lamb, and roasted poultry.

MEDIUM REDS Look to southern Europe for excellent Chiantis from Italy and Riojas from Spain to drink with pizza, pasta, and weeknight casseroles.

FULL-BODIED REDS Robust extracted wines, such as Zinfandel, Cabernet Sauvignon, Malbec, and Syrah, are go-tos for steaks, chops, roasts, and hearty stews.

SWEET WINES Late-harvest Sauternes, Riesling, Vin Santo, Muscat, and tawny port are delicious with figs and dried fruits, nuts, cheeses, and desserts.

how to hold a wineglass

If you grab a stemmed wineglass by the bowl, the warmth of your hand will warm up the liquid (which is okay if that's your intention), but your fingerprints may blur your view of the color and consistency of the wine. Instead, hold a wineglass by the stem while taking a sip.

To decant or not to decant

Pouring red wine into a specially designed decanter does two things: It develops flavor by aerating the wine, and it allows sediment to settle so it doesn't get into your glass. Aeration can benefit both younger and older wines, while sediment is generally present with older red wines and port.

pairing wine & food

Food and wine work best together when they share intensity—think of full-bodied red wine and rich meat dishes for example—or provide a study in contrasts, as with light, fruity white wine and spicy food.

serving beer

Twist off the cap and you're
done—there's no denying the
ease of serving up an ice-cold
beer. But if the occasion calls
for a bit more fanfare, try
specialty glassware beyond
the bottle, such as a tall glass
for Pilsner, a wide-mouth
goblet for Belgian-style ale,
or a handled stein for Irish stout.

All About Beer

Wine isn't the only drink that is both fun to sip and pair with food. Consider beer, too, especially with the huge range of microbrews and imported beers and ales available. It's a sociable drink that goes with shareable food, from a taco bar to a charcuterie plate to a seafood boil. There are no hard and fast rules about pairing, other than lighter, lager-style beers go with lighter foods and hearty brews with heartier dishes. To get to know more about beers and ales, find a store that stocks a wide variety and has a knowledgeable staff, then crack open a few bottles. It's a great assignment for the two of you to work on together.

BEER & FOOD PRIMER

All beers and ales are based on some combination of water, malt, hops, and yeast. Other ingredients, like herbs, spices, and fruits, can vary the flavor. Both beer and ale have light and dark versions, and there are literally hundreds of styles worldwide.

LAGERS Made by fermenting at relatively cool temperatures, lager has subtle flavors and a refreshing profile. Drink it with salty snacks and cured sausages and meats, as the Germans do, or with highly seasoned Mexican, Indian, and Asian food (it's fun to match the home country of the beer with the home country of the food). Pilsners and bocks are two of the most popular styles of lagers.

ALES Fermented at warmer temperatures than lager, ales have more robust spicy flavors and aromas. Belgian monasteries have a long tradition of brewing ales with unique fruits and herbs, and there are many Belgian styles, including whites, lambics, and Flemish reds. The ale family also includes pale ales, IPAs (India pale ales), porters, and stouts. Ales go with almost everything, from hamburgers to French onion soup to pizza.

DARK BEERS These can be ales, such as porters and stouts, or lagers, but the key is their nutty, caramel-like flavors that pair with strong cheeses, hearty stews, roasts, barbecued ribs, and even chocolate or caramelized desserts.

SOUR BEERS A subset of beer-making with a cult following, sour beers are intentionally tart and tangy and, for some, an acquired taste. The acidic edge makes pairing them with food a little more like pairing with wine.

CRAFT BEERS & MICROBREWS These come from independent producers experimenting in any of the above styles as well as crafting one-of-a-kind local, sometimes seasonal, brews. Because of the way they are made, these can be more perishable than mass-produced beers.

CHAPTER ONE

BREAKFAST & BRUNCH

What a joy to wake up with the one you love

wake up to doughnuts

There's no breakfast treat more heavenly than a batch
of crispy on the outside, fluffy on the inside, homemade
doughnuts. Choose from three scrumptious glazes.

Glazed Doughnuts

Few morning treats start the day off with more promise than a perfectly glazed doughnut. Don't be intimidated by the frying step; it's easier than you think. Make a few mimosas and a pot of coffee to sip alongside, and your perfect morning is complete.

MAKES 8–10 DOUGHNUTS AND HOLES

1 cup (8 fl oz/250 ml) whole milk, warmed (110°–120°F/43°–49°C)

1 package (2¼ tsp) instant yeast

3 Tbsp vegetable shortening, melted and cooled slightly

1 large egg

¼ cup (2 oz/60 g) sugar

2 tsp salt

3 cups (15 oz/470 g) all-purpose flour, plus more for dusting

Ultra Chocolate Glaze, Salted Caramel Glaze, or Meyer-Lemon Glaze with Pistachios (page 249)

Canola oil for greasing and frying

Pour the warm milk into a small bowl, sprinkle the yeast on top, and stir gently. Let stand in a warm spot until foamy, 5–10 minutes.

Transfer the yeast mixture to the bowl of a stand mixer fitted with the paddle attachment. Add the shortening, egg, sugar, salt, and 1½ cups (7½ oz/235 g) of the flour and beat on low speed until combined, about 2 minutes. Add the remaining 1½ cups flour, raise the speed to medium, and beat until incorporated, about 30 seconds. Switch to the dough hook and beat on medium speed until the dough is smooth and pulls away from the bowl, 3–4 minutes. Transfer to a well-oiled bowl, cover with a kitchen towel, and let the dough rise in a warm spot until doubled in size, about 1 hour.

Punch down the dough, turn it out onto a floured work surface, and roll out ½ inch (12 mm) thick. Using a doughnut cutter or 2 different-size round cutters (3½ inch/9 cm and 1 inch/2.5 cm), cut out doughnuts and holes. Transfer to a floured baking sheet, cover with a kitchen towel, and let rise in a warm spot until doubled in size, about 1 hour.

Meanwhile, make the glaze of choice. Set aside.

Pour oil to a depth of 2 inches (5 cm) into a deep-fryer or deep, heavy sauté pan and warm over medium-high heat until it reads 360°F (182°C) on a deep-frying thermometer. Carefully lower 2–5 doughnuts or holes into the hot oil and deep-fry until dark golden, about 1½ minutes. Turn over and cook until dark golden on the second side, about 1 minute longer. Transfer to a paper towel–lined baking sheet. Fry the remaining doughnuts and holes, allowing the oil to return to 360°F (182°C) between batches.

When the doughnuts and holes are cool enough to handle but still warm, dip all sides in the glaze, letting any excess drip into the bowl. Place on a wire rack until the glaze sets, about 30 minutes. Serve right away.

Orange, Olive Oil & Almond Cake

Even in those first few months after your introduction to wedded bliss, sometimes you just don't feel like sharing. Make this tender almond cake in two mini loaf pans and you can each have one to call your own. A citrusy yogurt glaze adds extra flavor and sweetness.

MAKES 1 LOAF CAKE, OR 2 MINI-LOAF CAKES; SERVES 12

Butter for greasing

1½ cups (7½ oz/235 g) all-purpose flour

2 tsp baking powder

½ tsp salt

½ cup (2½ oz/75 g) slivered blanched almonds

1 cup (8 oz/245 g) sugar

3 eggs

⅓ cup (3 fl oz/80 ml) olive oil

1 Tbsp minced orange zest

2 tsp vanilla extract

YOGURT GLAZE

½ cup powdered (icing) sugar

1 Tbsp plain Greek yogurt

¼ tsp minced orange zest

Preheat the oven to 350°F (180°C). Butter two 6-by-3-inch (15-by-8-cm) mini loaf pans or one 8-by-4-inch (20-by-10-cm) loaf pan. Line with parchment paper cut to cover the bottom and both sides, and butter the parchment. Dust with flour and shake out the excess.

In a bowl, stir together the flour, baking powder and salt. In a food processor, combine the almonds and ¼ cup (2 oz/60 g) of the sugar and process until finely ground. Add to the bowl with the flour mixture and stir to combine.

In a bowl, using an electric mixer, beat the eggs on medium-high speed until frothy. Increase the speed to high, add the remaining ¾ cup (6 oz/185 g) sugar and beat until thick and pale yellow, 6 to 8 minutes. Reduce the speed to low and beat in the olive oil, orange zest, and vanilla. Remove the bowl from the mixer. Using a spatula, gently fold in the flour-almond mixture until well blended. Scrape the batter into the prepared pans.

Bake the cake(s) until the top is golden brown and a skewer inserted into the center comes out clean, about 30 minutes. Transfer to a wire rack and let cool for 10 minutes. Run a thin-bladed knife around the edge of the pan(s), then invert the cake(s) to remove the pan(s). Turn upright on a wire rack and let cool while you prepare the glaze.

To make the yogurt glaze, in a small bowl, combine the powdered sugar, yogurt, and orange zest. Stir until blended and smooth. Spoon the glaze over the warm cake(s), letting it drizzle over the sides. Serve immediately, or let cool, cover, and refrigerate for up to 3 days.

Classic & Buttery Cream Scones

When toast and jam sounds too plain, make these rich, crumbly scones. The basic recipe is easy to vary. Currants or crystallized ginger are natural additions, but you can also try a mix of dried cherries and chocolate, lemon and lavender, or dried apricots and almonds.

MAKES 8 SCONES

2 cups (10 oz/315 g) all-purpose flour, plus more for dusting

3 Tbsp sugar

2½ tsp baking powder

¼ tsp sea salt

½ cup (4 oz/125 g) cold unsalted butter, cut into chunks, plus more for serving

Flavoring of choice (see suggestions below)

1 cup (8 fl oz/250 ml) heavy cream

FLAVORING SUGGESTIONS

Mix one of the following into the dry ingredients just before adding the cream:

1 tsp grated lemon zest and 1½ tsp fresh culinary lavender flowers

½ cup (3 oz/90 g) dried currants

½ cup (3 oz/90 g) crystallized ginger

½ cup (3 oz/90 g) *each* dried cherries and semisweet chocolate chunks

½ cup (3 oz/90 g) *each* dried apricots and slivered almonds

Preheat the oven to 400°F (200°C). Line a baking sheet with parchment paper. In a bowl, sift together the flour, sugar, baking powder, and salt. Using a pastry blender or 2 knives, cut the butter into the flour mixture just until the mixture forms large, coarse crumbs the size of peas. Add the flavoring of your choice. Pour the cream over the dry ingredients and stir with a fork or rubber spatula just until combined.

Turn the dough out onto a lightly floured work surface. Pat out into a circle about ½ inch (12 mm) thick. Using a 2½-inch (6-cm) biscuit cutter, cut out as many rounds of the dough as possible. Gather up the scraps, knead briefly, and continue patting and cutting out to make 8 scones. Place 1 inch (2.5 cm) apart on the prepared baking sheet.

Bake until golden brown, 17–20 minutes. Transfer to a wire rack and let cool slightly. Serve warm or at room temperature.

Smoothies & Juices

Green Smoothie

1 handful green grapes • ½ orange, peeled
and seeded • ½ lemon, peeled and seeded
½ cucumber, peeled, seeded, and diced
½ green apple, seeded and diced • 2 leaves
each kale and romaine lettuce, chopped
½ bunch fresh flat-leaf parsley leaves
½ cup (3 oz/90 g) frozen mango or pineapple
chunks • 7 or 8 ice cubes

In a blender, combine the grapes, orange,
lemon, cucumber, apple, kale, romaine,
parsley, mango, and ice cubes. Blend
on low for 10 seconds, then gradually
increase the speed to the highest setting
until smoothly puréed, about 1 minute.
Serve right away.

Mango Smoothie

1 mango, diced • 1 cup (8 fl oz/250 ml)
sweetened cranberry juice • 1 cup (8 oz/
250 g) plain nonfat yogurt • 3 or 4 ice cubes

In a blender, combine the mango,
cranberry juice, yogurt, and ice cubes.
Blend until frothy and thoroughly
blended. Serve right away.

Green Dream

1 Persian cucumber • 2 kiwis, peeled
1 lemon, peeled and seeded
1 green apple, quartered and cored
½ bunch kale, stems removed • ½ head
romaine lettuce, coarsely chopped

Cut the cucumber to fit a juicer.
Place the cucumber, kiwis, lemon,
apple, kale, and romaine into the
feeder of the juicer and run the
machine. Serve right away.

Freshly blended smoothies and juices make for a healthy and refreshing start to your day. The creamy beverages are quick to whip up whether you have a juicer or a blender, and are easily tailored to personal preference. Each recipe below makes enough to serve two.

Carrot-Pineapple

2 cups (12 oz/375 g) frozen pineapple chunks • ½ cup (4 fl oz/125 ml) carrot juice
1 cup (8 oz/250 g) plain nonfat yogurt
3 or 4 ice cubes

In a blender, combine the pineapple and carrot juice. Process until the mixture is smooth, 30–45 seconds. Add the yogurt and ice cubes and process until frothy and thoroughly blended, about 20 seconds longer. Serve right away.

Minty Pick-Me-Up

½ large pineapple • 1 pear, quartered and cored • 30 fresh mint leaves
1 cup (4 oz/12 g) hulled strawberries

Peel the pineapple. Cut the pineapple to fit a juicer or a blender. Place the pineapple, pear, mint, and strawberries into the feeder of the juicer or into the blender and run the machine. Serve right away.

Berry Smoothie

2 cups (8 oz/250 g) strawberries, hulls removed • 1 cup (4 oz/125 g) *each* blueberries and blackberries • 1 cup (8 oz/250 g) plain yogurt • 7 or 8 ice cubes
Agave nectar or honey

In a blender, combine the strawberries, blueberries, blackberries, yogurt, and ice cubes. Process until smooth, 30–45 seconds. Taste for sweetness and add a little agave if needed. Serve right away.

Whole-Grain Blueberry Muffins with Pecan Streusel

This recipe yields a dozen muffins, so you'll have plenty for future mornings on the go. Wrap them individually in aluminum foil, sealing tightly, and freeze them for up to 1 month. To serve, reheat, still wrapped, in a preheated 300°F (150°C) oven for about 20 minutes.

MAKES 12 MUFFINS

1 cup (3 oz/185 g) old-fashioned rolled oats

¾ cup (4 oz/125 g) whole-wheat flour

¾ cup (4 oz/125 g) all-purpose flour

⅓ cup (2½ oz/75 g) firmly packed brown sugar

2 tsp baking powder

½ tsp baking soda

½ tsp salt

1¼ cups (10 fl oz/310 ml) low-fat buttermilk

2 Tbsp canola oil

1 large egg

1 pint (8 oz/250 g) fresh blueberries (about 2 cups)

FOR THE STREUSEL

½ cup (2 oz/60 g) chopped pecans

2 tsp firmly packed brown sugar

2 tsp butter

Preheat the oven to 400°F (200°C). Line a 12-cup muffin pan with paper liners.

Place the oats in a food processor or blender and process until finely ground. Transfer to a bowl and add the flours, sugar, baking powder, baking soda, and salt. Whisk lightly to mix well. In a small bowl, whisk together the buttermilk, oil, and egg. Add the buttermilk mixture to the flour mixture and stir until blended. Gently stir in the blueberries.

To make the streusel, in another small bowl, mix the pecans, sugar, and butter. Using a fork or your fingers, rub lightly until evenly blended.

Spoon the batter evenly into the lined muffin cups. Sprinkle evenly with the streusel. Bake until a toothpick inserted into the center of a muffin comes out clean, about 22 minutes. Let cool in the pan on a wire rack for 5 minutes, then invert onto the rack, turn upright, and let cool completely.

Almond-Crusted French Toast with Raspberries

Challah is the ideal bread here because it readily absorbs the custard, creating an eggy, slightly sweet version of French toast reminiscent of the pain perdu *of New Orleans. Cap your breakfast for two with a café au lait, just as folks do in the Big Easy.*

SERVES 4

Canola oil for greasing

6 large eggs

1 cup (8 fl oz/250 ml) half-and-half

2 Tbsp sugar

Grated zest of 1 orange

¾ tsp almond extract (optional)

½ tsp vanilla extract

8 thick slices challah or other egg bread, preferably day-old

1 cup (4 oz/125 g) sliced almonds

1 cup (4 oz/125 g) fresh raspberries

Maple syrup, warmed, for serving

Preheat the oven to 350°F (180°C). Lightly oil 1 of 2 baking sheets.

In a large, shallow bowl, whisk together the eggs, half-and-half, sugar, orange zest, almond extract (if using), and vanilla. Add the bread slices, turning gently to coat evenly, and let soak until the bread has absorbed some of the egg mixture, about 1 minute.

Heat a griddle over medium heat until hot. Lightly oil the griddle. Spread the almonds on a plate. One piece at a time, remove the bread from the egg mixture, letting the excess egg mixture drip back into the bowl. Dip one side of the bread into the almonds, pressing gently to help the nuts adhere. Place each slice on the ungreased baking sheet.

Place the bread slices on the griddle, almond side down, and cook until the nuts begin to brown, about 2 minutes. Flip and cook until golden brown on the other side, about 2 minutes. Transfer to the greased baking sheet, almond side down, and bake until the center of the bread is heated through but still moist, about 10 minutes.

Serve topped with raspberries and drizzled with warmed maple syrup.

Raised Waffles with Strawberry-Rhubarb Compote

The batter for these extra-crisp, yeast-leavened waffles is quickly mixed the night before serving, so it is ready to pour into the waffle iron in the morning. Prepare the compote while the waffles are in the iron, or make it ahead and refrigerate, rewarming it just before serving.

SERVES 4

FOR THE COMPOTE

4 cups (1½ lb/750 g) coarsely chopped rhubarb stalks

¼ cup (2 oz/60 g) granulated sugar

1½ cups (6 oz/185 g) strawberries, hulled and halved

FOR THE WAFFLES

1 package (2¼ tsp) active dry yeast

1 tsp granulated sugar

¼ cup (2 fl oz/60 ml) warm water (105°–115°F/40°–46°C)

1 cup (8 fl oz/250 ml) whole milk

2 Tbsp butter

1 cup (5 oz/155 g) all-purpose flour

2 Tbsp firmly packed light brown sugar

¼ tsp salt

Canola or corn oil for brushing

1 large egg

¼ tsp baking soda

To make the strawberry-rhubarb compote, in a nonreactive saucepan over medium heat, combine the rhubarb, sugar, and ¼ cup (2 fl oz/60 ml) water. Cook until the mixture comes to a simmer and the rhubarb begins to release its liquid, about 10 minutes, then stir in the strawberries. Simmer gently until the rhubarb is soft when pierced with a fork, about 10 minutes. Skim any foam from the surface. Let cool, cover, and refrigerate the compote until serving.

To make the waffle batter, in a large bowl, dissolve the yeast and granulated sugar in the warm water and let stand until foamy, about 5 minutes. In a saucepan over low heat, combine the milk and butter and heat to lukewarm (about 115°F/46°C). In a small bowl, whisk together the flour, brown sugar, and salt. Stir the warm milk mixture into the dissolved yeast. Add the flour mixture and stir until blended. Cover the bowl and refrigerate overnight. The batter will thicken slightly.

Preheat the oven to 200°F (95°C). To cook the waffles, preheat a waffle iron for 5 minutes, then brush with oil. Add the egg and baking soda to the chilled batter and stir until blended. Ladle enough batter for 1 waffle into the center of the waffle iron (usually about ½ cup/4 fl oz/ 125 ml) and spread with a small spatula. Close the waffle iron and cook according to the manufacturer's directions or until the waffle is browned and crisp, usually 4–5 minutes. Transfer the waffle to a baking sheet and keep warm, uncovered, in the oven. Repeat with the remaining batter. Meanwhile, reheat the compote over low heat.

Serve the waffles warm with the warmed compote.

perfect harmony

The sweetness of strawberries
and the tartness of rhubarb
are the yin and yang of fruit
combinations. Together, they
offer a wonderful burst of
flavor and vibrant color to
a fruity compote for waffles.

The Best-Ever Banana Bread

Here's a great way to use up those bananas that went from sunny yellow to freckled with big brown spots before you knew it. Make the loaf at the beginning of the work week and cut a slice each morning for a quick and easily portable breakfast.

SERVES 8–10

½ cup (4 oz/125 g) unsalted butter, melted, plus more for greasing

2¼ cups (11½ oz/360 g) all-purpose flour, plus more for dusting

1 cup (8 oz/250 g) sugar

1 tsp baking soda

½ tsp salt

3 very ripe bananas

2 large eggs, lightly beaten

⅓ cup (3 oz/90 g) plain yogurt

1 tsp vanilla extract

1 cup (4 oz/125 g) walnuts, chopped (optional)

Preheat the oven to 350°F (180°C). Butter and flour a 5-by-9-inch (13-by-23-cm) loaf pan. In a bowl, mix together the flour, sugar, baking soda, and salt. In a large bowl, mash the bananas with a fork. Add the melted butter, eggs, yogurt, and vanilla. Stir until blended. Gradually add the flour mixture to the banana mixture, stirring gently just until combined. Stir in the nuts, if using. Scrape the batter into the prepared loaf pan.

Bake until a toothpick inserted into the center comes out clean, about 1 hour. If the top begins to brown too much during baking, cover loosely with aluminum foil. Let the pan cool on a wire rack for 10 minutes, then turn the bread out onto the rack, turn right side up, and let cool completely. Cut the bread into slices and serve at room temperature. Wrap any leftover bread in plastic wrap and store at room temperature for up to 5 days.

Nut & Seed Maple Power Bars

For breakfast-to-go, choose these nutty homemade granola bars made with thick-cut oats, an abundance of raw seeds and nuts, and maple syrup. Mashing the dates well will help to hold the baked bars together. When baking, let the oats turn dark brown for the best flavor.

MAKES 8 BARS

Canola oil for greasing

2 cups (6 oz/185 g) old-fashioned rolled oats

½ cup (2½ oz/75 g) raw almonds, coarsely chopped

½ cup (2 oz/60 g) raw pumpkin seeds

½ cup (2 oz/60 g) raw sunflower seeds

2 Tbsp flaxseeds

½ tsp salt

¾ cup (7½ oz/235 g) dark maple syrup

6 Medjool dates, pitted and chopped

2 Tbsp coconut oil

Preheat the oven to 350°F (180°C). Oil an 8-inch (20-cm) square baking pan. Line the pan with parchment paper, allowing the paper to overhang the edge on two opposite sides, and oil the paper inside the pan.

In a mixing bowl, combine the oats, almonds, pumpkin seeds, sunflower seeds, flaxseeds, and salt. Set aside.

In a small pot over medium-high heat, combine the maple syrup and dates and bring to a boil. Reduce the heat and boil gently, stirring occasionally, until the dates are soft and the syrup is slightly thickened, 8–10 minutes. Off the heat, using a fork, mix in the coconut oil and mash the dates until the syrup is pulpy, about 2 minutes; there should be about 1 cup (11 oz/345 g) of syrup.

Add the syrup to the oat mixture and mix with a spatula until well coated. Spread the mixture in the prepared pan, using the back of the spatula to firmly press it into an even 1-inch (2.5-cm) layer.

Bake the bar slab until the top is dark brown and the mixture is firm around the edges and yields only slightly when pressed with your finger in the center of the pan, about 50 minutes. Cool in the pan on a wire rack for 1 hour, then turn out onto the rack and let cool completely. Using a serrated knife, cut into 8 bars. Store, wrapped in aluminum foil, at room temperature for up to 5 days.

Fresh Fruit Pop Tarts

This rendition of the decades-old favorite has all the crispy pastry and sweet appeal of the original palm-size pastry, but with the added punch of a fresh fruit filling. Enjoy the tarts at room temperature, or lay them flat on a baking sheet and reheat in a low oven.

SERVES 4

1½ cups (7½ oz/235 g) plus 2 Tbsp all-purpose flour, plus more for dusting

Pinch of salt

½ cup (4 oz/125 g) plus 1 Tbsp unsalted butter, cut into pieces

¼ cup (2 fl oz/60 ml) ice water

1½ cups (about 8 oz/250 g) fresh blackberries or blueberries or 2 peaches or nectarines, peeled and pitted

2 Tbsp granulated sugar

1 egg white

FOR THE VANILLA GLAZE

¾ cup (3 oz/95 g) plus 2 Tbsp confectioners' sugar

2½ Tbsp water

½ tsp vanilla extract

To make the pastry, in a bowl, mix the 1½ cups flour and salt. Scatter the butter pieces over the flour. Using a pastry blender or two knives, cut in the butter into until pea-size clumps form. Mix in the ice water. Gently knead the dough against the side of the bowl until it begins to hold together. Wrap in plastic wrap and refrigerate for 1 hour.

Finely chop the fruit, transfer to a bowl, and stir in the sugar. Let stand for at least 10 minutes or up to 1 hour.

Preheat the oven to 375°F (190°C). Line a baking sheet with parchment paper. Place the egg white in a cup for brushing.

Stir the 2 tablespoons flour into the berries. On a lightly floured board, roll out the dough into a long rectangle about 9 by 16 inches (23 by 33 cm). Using a knife, trim the dough into a 12-by-15-inch (30-by-38-cm) rectangle, then into six 4-by-5-inch (10-by-13-cm) rectangles. Gather the dough scraps into a flat disk, wrap in plastic wrap, and refrigerate.

Place 2 of the dough rectangles on the prepared baking sheet. Brush the perimeter of 1 rectangle with the egg white. Spoon one-fourth of the fruit mixture onto the dough, leaving a ½-inch (12-mm) border uncovered. Using a knife, cut vents into the top of the second rectangle and carefully place it over the first one, sealing the fruit inside. Using the tines of a fork, crimp the edges shut. Repeat to form 2 more fruit pop tarts and refrigerate on the baking sheet. Use the dough scraps and remaining fruit to make 1 more pop tart. Place on the baking sheet with the other pop tarts and refrigerate for 15 minutes.

Bake until golden brown, about 25 minutes. Let cool.

To make the vanilla glaze, in a small bowl, blend the confectioners' sugar, water, and vanilla until smooth.

Drizzle the glaze evenly over the tarts and serve.

MODERN
HEIRLOOM

something blue

Blueberries are an ideal
addition to warmed maple
syrup because they expand
and pop when heated,
releasing lots of their fruity
juices. Add nuts and seeds
to the batter for pancakes
with extra crunch or bananas
for flavor.

Blueberry Buttermilk Pancakes

Blueberries are nutritional powerhouses—loaded with antioxidants and high in vitamins C and K and in manganese—which makes these delicious pancakes good for you. Stack the leftovers, separated with waxed paper, in an airtight container and refrigerate for up to 4 days, then reheat in a microwave or toaster oven.

MAKES ABOUT 10 PANCAKES; SERVES 2–3

1½ cups (7½ oz/235 g) all-purpose flour

2 Tbsp sugar

1½ tsp baking powder

¾ tsp baking soda

¼ tsp salt

1¾ cups (14 fl oz/430 ml) buttermilk, plus more as needed

2 large eggs

3 Tbsp unsalted butter, melted, plus more, at room temperature, for serving

2 cups (8 oz/250 g) fresh blueberries

Canola oil for frying

Maple syrup, warmed, for serving

Preheat the oven to 200°F (95°C). In a large bowl, sift together the flour, sugar, baking powder, baking soda, and salt. In a bowl, whisk together the buttermilk, eggs, and melted butter. Pour the buttermilk mixture into the flour mixture and stir just until combined. Fold in the blueberries.

Heat a griddle over high heat until a drop of water flicked on the surface sizzles and immediately evaporates. Lightly oil the griddle. Ladle about ¼ cup (2 fl oz/60 ml) of the batter onto the griddle for each pancake and cook until bubbles form on the surface, about 2 minutes. Flip the pancakes and cook until the bottoms are golden brown, about 1 minute longer. Transfer to a baking sheet and keep warm in the oven. Repeat with the remaining batter. If the batter begins to thicken, thin with a bit more buttermilk.

Serve the warm pancakes with butter and maple syrup.

blueberry syrup

To dress up the maple syrup—and enjoy a double dose of berries—gently simmer 2 cups (8 oz/250 g) fresh blueberries with 1 cup (11 oz/345 g) maple syrup in a saucepan until the berries start to release their juices, about 5 minutes. Serve warm.

pancake variations

NUT & SEED Add 1 teaspoon poppy seeds, 1 tablespoon sesame seeds, and 1 tablespoon chopped pecans to the batter.

BANANA Add 1 mashed banana to the batter.

Classic French Crepes

These thin, delicate pancakes can be filled, sauced, or spread with a variety of ingredients, such as jam or marmalade, chocolate-hazelnut spread, or sliced fruit and mascarpone cheese. To make savory crepes, omit the sugar and vanilla and add a pinch of salt, then fill the crepes with scrambled eggs and bacon or ham and cheese.

SERVES 4

½ cup (4 fl oz/125 ml) whole milk

2 large eggs

1 cup (5 oz/155 g) all-purpose flour

2 tsp sugar

1 tsp vanilla extract

Melted unsalted butter for brushing

In a blender, combine ½ cup (4 fl oz/125 ml) water with the milk, eggs, flour, sugar, and vanilla. Blend until very smooth and free of lumps. Cover and refrigerate for at least 1 hour or up to 1 day.

Using a pastry brush dipped in the melted butter, lightly grease the entire surface of a 9-inch (23-cm) crepe pan or nonstick frying pan and place over medium heat. Holding the pan at an angle above the burner, ladle about ¼ cup (2 fl oz/60 ml) of batter into the pan close to one edge. Quickly swirl the pan so that the batter covers the entire bottom of the pan. Cook, shaking the pan from time to time, until the crepe begins to bubble, the bottom is lightly browned, and the batter looks set, about 1 minute. Use a small spatula to lift the edge of the crepe, then carefully grasp the edge and quickly flip over in the pan. Cook for another 10 seconds, until the second side is slightly browned and set. Transfer the finished crepe to a plate and cover with a square of waxed paper. Repeat with the remaining batter, stacking the crepes on the plate between squares of waxed paper.

Nectarine-Almond Oven Pancake

Also known as a "Dutch baby," this skillet pancake inflates dramatically in the oven, and falls rapidly once removed from the heat. Serve it straight from the frying pan, piled with summer nectarines and sliced almonds and dusted with confectioners' sugar. Kitchen shears make an easy task of cutting into the pan-size pancake.

SERVES 4

½ cup (2½ oz/75 g) all-purpose flour

1 Tbsp granulated sugar

½ tsp salt

6 Tbsp (3 oz/90 g) unsalted butter

½ cup (4 fl oz/125 ml) whole milk

3 large eggs, beaten

3 ripe nectarines or peaches, pitted and sliced (about 4 cups/24 oz/750 g)

2 Tbsp firmly packed light brown sugar

2 tsp fresh lemon juice

¼ cup (1 oz/30 g) lightly toasted sliced almonds

Confectioners' sugar for serving

fruit variations

Use any fruit that's in season. Try blueberries, raspberries, and blackberries in summer, or apples and pears in autumn.

Preheat the oven to 375°F (190°C).

In a bowl, mix the flour, granulated sugar, and salt.

In a 10-inch (25-cm) ovenproof frying pan, add 4 tablespoons (2 oz/60 g) of the butter. Heat in the oven until the butter is melted, about 2 minutes. Reserve half of the melted butter and leave the remaining butter in the pan.

Make a well in the center of the flour mixture and pour in the milk, eggs, and reserved melted butter. Whisk just until combined. Pour into the hot frying pan.

Return to the oven and bake until the edges of the pancake are puffed and golden brown, about 20 minutes.

Meanwhile, in another frying pan, melt the remaining 2 tablespoons butter over medium heat. Add the nectarines, brown sugar, and lemon juice and cook, stirring occasionally, until the nectarines have given off their juices and the brown sugar has melted, about 3 minutes. Remove from the heat.

Remove the pan from the oven. Pour the nectarine mixture into the center of the pancake. Sprinkle with the almonds and dust lightly with confectioners' sugar. Cut into wedges and serve hot, directly from the pan.

granola

almonds

pecans

freeze-dried
strawberries

candied
ginger

pumpkin
seeds

golden
raisins

flaked
coconut

walnuts

Granola Five Ways

Store-bought granola just can't compare to homemade. Start with one great recipe, then modify it according to your own preferences. Try any of the variations suggested here, or experiment with your own combinations.

basic granola

2½ cups (7½ oz/220 g) old-fashioned rolled oats

1 cup (5 oz/175 g) sliced almonds

½ cup (2 oz/60 g) puffed rice cereal

½ cup (2 oz/60 g) raw seeds

½ cup (2½ oz/75 g) lightly packed brown sugar

¾ teaspoon *each* salt and ground cinnamon

½ cup (4 fl oz/125 ml) coconut oil or canola oil

1 teaspoon almond extract

1 large egg white, beaten until frothy

½ cup (2½ oz/80 g) golden raisins or currants

Preheat the oven to 350°F (180°C). Line a rimmed baking sheet with parchment paper.

In a large bowl, combine the oats, almonds, cereal, seeds, brown sugar, salt, and cinnamon and mix well. In a small bowl, whisk together the oil and extract. Pour the oil mixture over the oat mixture. Add the egg white and toss gently to combine.

Pour the mixture onto the prepared baking sheet, spreading it into a single layer. Bake, stirring once or twice, until the mixture is nicely toasted, about 35 minutes. Let cool. Stir in the dried fruit just before serving or storing. Store in an airtight container at room temperature for up to 1 month.

MAKES ABOUT 6½ CUPS (40 OZ/1.25 KG)

banana + walnut

walnuts

unsweetened flaked coconut

ground cinnamon

ground nutmeg

rum extract

broken banana chips

To the oats, add walnuts in place of the almonds and unsweetened flaked coconut in place of the rice cereal. Omit the seeds. Add the brown sugar, salt, cinnamon, and ¼ teaspoon ground nutmeg. Add the oil with rum extract in place of the almond extract. Add the egg white. Add banana chips in place of the raisins.

maple + pecan

pecans

puffed rice cereal

maple syrup

ground cinnamon

ground ginger

To the oats, add pecans in place of the almonds. Add the cereal and omit the seeds. Substitute maple syrup for the brown sugar. Add the salt, decrease the cinnamon to ½ teaspoon, and add ½ teaspoon ground ginger. Add the oil with almond extract in place of the vanilla extract. Add the egg white. Omit the raisins.

ginger + pumpkin seed

unsweetened flaked coconut

pumpkin seeds

ground cinnamon

ground ginger

crystallized ginger

To the oats and almonds, add unsweetened flaked coconut in place of the rice cereal. Add pumpkin seeds for the seeds. Add the salt, decrease the cinnamon to ½ teaspoon, and add ½ teaspoon ground ginger. Substitute almond extract for the vanilla extract. Add the egg white. Add ½ cup (3 oz/90 g) crystallized ginger in addition to the golden raisins.

strawberry + almond

almonds

sesame seeds

ground cinnamon

ground nutmeg

almond extract

freeze-dried strawberries

To the oats, almonds, and cereal, add sesame seeds for the seeds. Add the sugar, salt, cinnamon, and ¼ teaspoon ground nutmeg. Add the oil and almond extract. Add the egg white. Substitute 1 cup (3 oz/90 g) freeze-dried strawberries for the raisins.

Steel-Cut Oats with Honeyed Pears

Sit down to a bowl of chewy yet tender oatmeal, and you will begin to crave it regularly. That's partly because here it's dressed up with fancy pears and nuts, but it's also because you know that steel-cut oats are rich in dietary fiber, good fuel for a healthy heart.

SERVES 4

¼ tsp salt

1 cup (6 oz/185 g) steel-cut oats

1 Tbsp plus 1 tsp unsalted butter

½ cup (2 oz/60 g) pecans

2 tsp sugar

2 ripe, juicy pears such as Comice or Anjou, peeled, cored, and cut into chunks

3 Tbsp honey

¼ tsp ground cinnamon

Half-and-half, cream, or milk for serving

variation

APPLES & CRYSTALLIZED GINGER
Substitute Golden Delicious apples for the pears. Add a sprinkling of minced crystallized ginger when topping the oats.

In a heavy saucepan over high heat, bring 4 cups (32 fl oz/1 l) water and the salt to a boil. Stir in the oats and return to a boil. Reduce the heat to medium-low and simmer uncovered, stirring frequently to avoid scorching, until the oats are done to your preferred texture, 25–35 minutes.

In a frying pan, melt the 1 teaspoon butter over medium heat. Add the pecans and sprinkle with the sugar. Cook, stirring constantly, until the sugar melts and the pecans are toasted and glazed, about 1 minute. Transfer to a chopping board. Let the pecans cool slightly, then coarsely chop. Rinse out the frying pan.

Just before the oats are done, melt the 1 tablespoon butter over medium heat in the frying pan. Add the pears and cook, stirring occasionally, until they give off some juices and are heated through, about 3 minutes. Add the honey and cinnamon and stir just until the honey melts.

Spoon the oats into bowls. Top with the pears and their juices and the pecans. Drizzle with half-and-half and serve.

Fried Egg & Bacon Breakfast Panini

Here, a classic morning combo is taken to the next level with the use of a sandwich press. English muffins or slices from a crusty whole-wheat loaf are the bread of choice, though any dense loaf will work. Add a dash of hot-pepper sauce at the table.

SERVES 2

4 thick slices bacon

2 Tbsp unsalted butter, at room temperature

2 large eggs

2 tsp chopped fresh tarragon

Salt and freshly ground pepper

2 English muffins, split in half, or 4 slices coarse whole-wheat country bread, each about ½ inch (12 mm) thick

2 oz (60 g) Cheddar cheese, thinly sliced

In a frying pan over medium heat, cook the bacon until crisp, 6–8 minutes. Transfer to paper towels to drain. Pour off the fat from the pan.

In the same frying pan, melt 1 tablespoon of the butter. When the butter is hot and foamy, crack the eggs into the pan. Cook over medium heat until the whites are set with crisped brown edges and the yolks begin to firm around the edges, 3–4 minutes. Sprinkle with the tarragon and season with salt and pepper. Flip the eggs and cook until the yolks are softly set, about 30 seconds more.

Meanwhile, preheat the sandwich grill. Spread both sides of each muffin half with the remaining 1 tablespoon butter. Place the muffins, cut sides up, on the grill, close the top plate, and cook until lightly toasted, 1–2 minutes. On the bottom half of each muffin, layer one-fourth of the cheese, 1 fried egg, and 2 bacon slices. Divide the remaining cheese equally on top. Cover with the muffin tops, cut sides down, and press gently. Close the top plate and cook until the muffins are golden and toasted and the cheese is melted, 4–5 minutes. Serve right away.

Yogurt Parfait Jars

If there is power in simplicity and perfect partnerships, this easy breakfast-in-a-jar delivers big, providing a healthy dose of energy that will carry you to lunchtime. Mix it in the morning or make it the night before for an easily transportable breakfast on the run.

SERVES 2

½ cup (2½ oz/75 g) fresh raspberries or chopped fresh strawberries

1 Tbsp honey

½ tsp vanilla extract

1 cup (8 oz/250 g) plain Greek yogurt

½ cup (2½ oz/75 g) granola (purchased or homemade, see pages 48–49)

½ cup (2½ oz/75 g) blueberries or blackberries

In a small bowl, combine the raspberries, honey, and vanilla. Mash with the back of a fork until chunky and well mixed. Divide the berry mixture equally between two pint-size jars, spoon the yogurt on top, then layer each one equally with the granola and blueberries.

Eat at once, or cover and refrigerate for up to 1 day.

Chia Pudding Jars

Chia seeds are tiny whole grains that carry a big nutritional punch. Here, they are made into a simple breakfast pudding topped with fruit. You can mix up extra pudding bases and store them for up to 3 days, then top them as needed before heading out the door.

SERVES 2

½ cup (4 fl oz/125 ml) almond milk, coconut milk, or a combination

2 Tbsp chia seeds

3 tsp maple syrup

2 dashes vanilla extract

2 cups (10 oz/315 g) diced mango, blueberries, or sliced strawberries, or a combination

2 Tbsp toasted coconut chips

Use two pint-size jars. In each jar, stir together ¼ cup (2 fl oz/60 ml) almond milk, 1 tablespoon chia seeds, 1½ teaspoons maple syrup, and a dash of vanilla extract. Cover and refrigerate at least 4 hours or overnight.

Stir the chia mixture and set aside at room temperature until the seeds are plumped, about 10 minutes. When the seeds are evenly plumped, layer the fruit on top. Sprinkle each jar evenly with toasted coconut. Use a long spoon to dig right in, or screw the lid onto each jar for a breakfast on the go.

Nothing starts the day off right like a breakfast jar packed with vitamins and nutrients. Once you get the hang of the basic method, try your own variations on the theme, adding different types of fresh fruits and experimenting with nuts, seeds, and dried fruits for extra flavor. You can also swap out the almond milk and plump the chia seeds in orange or apple juice, or a fruit nectar.

INTIMATE MORNINGS

Lingering over a delicious homemade breakfast
and a second cup of coffee is a weekend luxury, and dishes
like almond-crusted French toast or savory quiche
make it especially indulgent. But even on busy mornings
you can sneak in special time together before setting
out to conquer the day. Whether you wake up to fruity
smoothies and easy yogurt parfaits or to your own
favorite mix of crunchy granola, there are plenty
of tasty ways to rise and shine together.

Bacon, Leek & Gruyère Quiche

Baked in a tart pan, this cheesy, bacon-studded quiche is a leaner and more refined version of the familiar favorite. Serve it alongside a salad of mixed greens and mimosas for a lazy mid-day brunch.

SERVES 6

Single-Crust Flaky Pie Dough
(page 250)

4 thick slices applewood–smoked bacon, coarsely chopped

1 Tbsp unsalted butter

2 small leeks, including tender green tops, chopped

1 cup (8 fl oz/250 ml) half-and-half

2 large eggs

½ tsp salt

¼ tsp freshly ground pepper

⅛ tsp freshly grated nutmeg

1 cup (4 oz/125 g) shredded Gruyère cheese

variation

HAM, SHALLOT & CHEDDAR
In a frying pan, cook 1 cup (5 oz/ 155 g) chopped smoked ham in 1 tablespoon butter over medium heat until heated through, about 3 minutes. Add ⅓ cup (2 oz/60 g) chopped shallots and cook until tender, about 2 minutes. Substitute the ham mixture for the leeks and bacon and use shredded sharp Cheddar cheese for the Gruyère.

Place the dough on a lightly floured work surface and dust the top with flour. Roll out into a round 12 inches (30 cm) in diameter and about ⅛ (3 mm) inch thick. Transfer to a 9-inch (23-cm) tart pan with a removable bottom, fitting the dough into the bottom and sides of the pan. Using scissors or a small knife, trim the dough, leaving a ½-inch (12 mm) overhang. Fold the overhanging dough into the pan, pressing it firmly against the dough on the sides of the pan; the dough should be doubly thick at the sides and rise about ⅛ inch (3 mm) above the rim. Line the dough with a piece of aluminum foil and freeze for 30 minutes.

Meanwhile, position a rack in the lower third of the oven and preheat to 375°F (190°C). Place the tart pan on a baking sheet and fill with pie weights or dried beans. Bake until the dough sets and begins to brown, 15–20 minutes.

Meanwhile, in a frying pan, fry the bacon over medium heat, stirring, until crisp and golden, about 6 minutes. Using a slotted spoon, transfer to paper towels to drain. Pour out the fat in the pan and wipe the pan with paper towels. Add the butter to the pan and melt over medium heat. Add the leeks and cook, stirring occasionally, until tender, about 10 minutes. Transfer to a plate and let cool slightly.

Remove the baking sheet with the tart pan from the oven. Remove the foil and its contents. In a bowl, whisk together the half-and-half, eggs, salt, pepper, and nutmeg until combined. Scatter the leeks, bacon, and Gruyère evenly in the pastry shell. Pour the egg mixture into the shell. Return to the oven and bake until the filling is puffed and golden brown, about 30 minutes.

Transfer the pan to a wire rack and let cool until warm, about 30 minutes. Remove the sides of the pan, cut the quiche into wedges, and serve warm or at room temperature.

Swiss Chard, Onion & Cheese Frittata

Try your favorite olive varieties in this delicious frittata. Any one you choose will add a mellow, salty appeal to this dish. Place any leftover frittata in an airtight container in the refrigerator for up to 2 days. Bring to room temperature or reheat before serving.

SERVES 6–8

1 bunch Swiss chard (about 1¼ lb/625 g)

4 Tbsp (2 fl oz/60 ml) olive oil

1 small yellow onion, thinly sliced

Salt and freshly ground black pepper

6 large eggs

4 cloves garlic, finely chopped

¼ cup (1 oz/30 g) grated hard cheese such as Parmesan

Pinch of cayenne pepper

make it your own

You can mix into a frittata almost anything you would use as a filling in a folded omelet or a quiche. Try thinly sliced zucchini; ham and sharp white Cheddar; shredded mozzarella and cherry tomatoes mixed with garlic and thyme; or diced red bell pepper, yellow onion, sausage, and feta cheese. Brown any meats and parboil or sauté any vegetables before combining them with the eggs.

Position a rack in the upper third of the oven and preheat to 350°F (180°C). Cut the chard stems crosswise into slices ¼ inch (6 mm) thick. Coarsely chop the leaves.

In a large frying pan over medium heat, warm 2 tablespoons of the olive oil. Add the onion and sauté until tender, about 6 minutes. Add the chard stems, season with salt, and sauté for about 4 minutes. Add the chopped leaves and sauté until tender, 2–3 minutes. Transfer to a plate. Set aside.

In a large bowl, lightly beat the eggs with the garlic and cheese. Season with the cayenne, salt, and black pepper.

Gently squeeze the liquid from the chard. Add the chard to the egg mixture and stir until blended. In an 8-inch (20-cm) ovenproof frying pan over medium-high heat, warm the remaining 2 tablespoons olive oil. Add the egg-chard mixture, reduce the heat to medium, and cook until the eggs are set around the edges, about 5 minutes. Transfer to the oven and cook until set in the center, 7–9 minutes longer. Let cool briefly.

If desired, invert the frittata onto a large plate. Cut into wedges and serve.

keep it green

Asparagus isn't the only green vegetable
that would feature well in this dish. Swap out
the tender spears for other verdant vegetables
in season. Try sautéed spinach or kale,
broccolini, or green beans instead.

Fried Eggs with Asparagus, Pancetta & Bread Crumbs

With its salty pancetta, crispy bread crumbs, and sweet roasted asparagus, this fried egg dish boasts the perfect marriage of complementary ingredients. If it's just the two of you for breakfast, cut this recipe in half, since it's best enjoyed hot from the frying pan.

SERVES 4

4 slices white bread

Salt and freshly ground pepper

¼ tsp finely chopped fresh thyme or rosemary

16 asparagus spears, tough ends removed

Olive oil for drizzling

2 tsp unsalted butter, plus 2 Tbsp

2 thin slices pancetta, chopped

4 large eggs

Freshly grated Parmesan cheese for garnish (optional)

Cut the crusts off the bread slices and discard. Tear the bread into pieces. In a food processor, combine the bread pieces and a pinch each of salt and pepper. Process to form coarse crumbs. Add the thyme or rosemary and pulse a few times, just until well mixed. You should have 1 cup (2 oz/60 g). (The crumbs can be stored in an airtight container in the freezer for up to 6 months.)

Preheat the oven to 400°F (200°C).

Spread the asparagus in a baking dish large enough to hold it in a single layer. Drizzle with the oil and season with salt and pepper. Turn the spears to coat them evenly. Roast, turning once or twice, until tender-crisp and the color has darkened slightly, about 15 minutes; the timing will depend on the thickness of the spears. Remove from the oven and cover loosely with aluminum foil.

In a small frying pan, melt the 2 teaspoons butter over medium-high heat. Add the pancetta and sauté just until it darkens slightly, about 1 minute. Add the bread crumbs and sauté until golden, about 2 minutes. Remove from the heat.

In a large frying pan, melt the 2 tablespoons butter over medium-high heat. Break the eggs into the pan, spacing them about 1 inch (2.5 cm) apart. Reduce the heat to low and season the eggs with salt and pepper. Cover and cook until the whites are set and the yolks begin to firm around the edges, 5–7 minutes.

Just before the eggs are ready, arrange the asparagus on plates. Transfer the eggs to the plates. Sprinkle the eggs and asparagus with the bread crumb mixture. Garnish with Parmesan cheese, if using, and serve.

Eggs Baked in Tomatoes

This recipe is perfect for a late breakfast on a weekend morning when you don't want to spend much time at the stove but do want something simple and elegant. If you like, toast thin slices of pain au levain, *drizzle with olive oil, and serve the tomatoes atop the bread.*

SERVES 2

2 ripe but firm tomatoes

Salt and freshly ground pepper

2 large eggs

2 Tbsp freshly grated Parmesan cheese, preferably Parmigiano-Reggiano

1½ tsp extra-virgin olive oil

2 Tbsp fresh basil leaves, cut into thin ribbons

Preheat the oven to 450°F (230°C). Line a rimmed baking sheet with aluminum foil.

Using a serrated knife, cut off the top one-fourth of each tomato. Using the tip of a spoon, carefully hollow out the tomatoes, leaving a cup about ½ inch (12 mm) thick. Discard the tomato seeds or reserve for another use. Place the tomato cups on the prepared baking sheet and sprinkle the insides with a pinch each of salt and pepper.

Carefully crack an egg into each tomato and sprinkle 1 tablespoon of the Parmesan over each egg. Place the baking sheet in the oven and bake until the egg whites are set and the yolks have begun to thicken but are still a bit runny, 8–10 minutes.

Remove the egg-stuffed tomatoes from the oven. Drizzle the tops with olive oil and scatter evenly with the basil. Place each tomato on a plate and serve right away.

Huevos Rancheros with Tomato Sauce

This type of hearty dish—with crisp fried tortillas, eggs, and tomato sauce—is traditional mid-morning fare on rural Mexican farms and lends its rejuvenating nature to lazy weekend mornings. Cubed papaya with a squeeze of lime is a nice accompaniment.

SERVES 4

FOR THE ROASTED TOMATO SAUCE

7 ripe plum tomatoes, cored

2–3 serrano chiles, seeded and minced

½ small onion, chopped

1 large clove garlic, chopped

1 Tbsp grapeseed or canola oil

Salt

4 whole-wheat tortillas

Grapeseed or canola oil for frying

4 large eggs

Salt and freshly ground pepper

1 cup (8 oz/250 g) canned fat-free refried black beans, warmed

1 small ripe avocado, pitted, peeled, and sliced

⅓ cup (1½ oz/45 g) crumbled feta or cotija cheese

⅔ cup (5 oz/155 g) plain nonfat Greek yogurt

1 Tbsp coarsely chopped fresh cilantro

To make the tomato sauce, in a dry frying pan over high heat, roast the tomatoes, turning them as they char slightly, about 5 minutes. Transfer to a food processor and add the chiles, onion, and garlic. Process until blended but still chunky. In a large frying pan over medium-high heat, warm the oil. Add the tomato mixture and cook, stirring constantly, until thickened, about 5 minutes. Taste and adjust the seasoning with salt. Keep warm.

Preheat the oven to 200°F (95°C). Wrap the tortillas in aluminum foil and keep warm in the oven.

Coat a large frying pan with a thin film of oil and warm the oil over medium-low heat. Carefully break the eggs into the pan and fry slowly until the whites are set and the yolks have begun to thicken but are not hard, about 3 minutes. Cover the frying pan, if you like firm yolks. Season with salt and pepper.

To assemble, remove the tortillas from the oven. Using tongs, dip each tortilla quickly in the warm tomato sauce and place on warmed individual plates. Spread ¼ cup (2 oz/60 g) of the refried beans evenly on each tortilla and top each with a fried egg. Spoon more of the tomato sauce generously over the eggs. Top with the avocado, cheese, yogurt, and cilantro. Serve right away.

California Breakfast Bowls

To save time in the morning, cook the quinoa and tomatoes and mix the sauce the night before. At breakfast time, reheat the quinoa with a splash of water, and you'll be eating in just minutes.

SERVES 2

FOR THE YOGURT SAUCE

¼ cup (2 oz/60 g) plain yogurt

1 tsp grated lemon zest

1 Tbsp fresh lemon juice

Salt and freshly ground pepper

1 pint grape tomatoes

2 tsp extra-virgin olive oil

Salt and freshly ground pepper

¾ cup (6 oz/185 g) golden quinoa

¼ cup (1 oz/30 g) crumbled feta cheese

Olive oil for frying

2 large eggs

½ ripe avocado, pitted, peeled, and thinly sliced

1½ oz (45 g) broccoli sprouts or other sprouts

4 tsp toasted uncooked buckwheat groats

To make the yogurt sauce, in a small bowl, whisk together the yogurt and lemon zest and juice. Season with salt and pepper. Set aside.

Preheat the oven to 425°F (220°C). Place the tomatoes on a rimmed baking sheet, drizzle with the oil, and stir to coat. Season with salt and pepper. Roast the tomatoes, stirring once halfway through roasting, until slightly wrinkled but not collapsed, about 20 minutes total. Let cool.

While the tomatoes are roasting, rinse the quinoa in a fine-mesh sieve, then transfer wet to a saucepan. Place over medium-high heat and cook the quinoa, stirring often, until fragrant and starting to pop, 4–5 minutes. Remove from the heat and add 2 cups (16 fl oz/500 ml) water; it will spatter. Add a pinch of salt, return to the heat, and bring to a boil. Cover, reduce the heat to medium-low, and simmer until all of the liquid has been absorbed and the quinoa is almost tender, about 15 minutes. Remove from the heat and let stand, covered, for 10 minutes.

Fluff the quinoa with a fork and divide between two wide, shallow bowls, Spoon half of the yogurt sauce over the quinoa in each bowl, then sprinkle with half of the feta.

In a frying pan over medium-high heat, warm a small amount of oil. Break the eggs into the pan, spacing them about 1 inch (2.5 cm) apart. Reduce the heat to medium and cook until the whites are set and the yolks are nearly set, 5–7 minutes. Using a metal spatula, place an egg to one side of the quinoa in each bowl.

Arrange half of the avocado slices along one edge of each bowl with half of the roasted tomatoes. Arrange a generous pinch of sprouts on another edge of each bowl. Top each bowl with a sprinkle of buckwheat and serve right away.

super bowls

With eggs and quinoa for protein, avocados for potassium and heart-healthy fatty acids, and tomatoes for vitamin C and antioxidants (plus Greek yogurt, sprouts, and groats), these nourishing bowls will superfood-charge your day.

Classic Two-Egg Omelets

On weekday mornings, you want something that's hot and satisfying but requires minimal work and fuss. Omelets are simple to prepare and easily adapt to any variety of inspired filling combinations.

SERVES 2

4 large eggs

Salt

2 Tbsp butter

Filling of choice (see suggestions below)

filling variations

The choices of omelet fillings are limitless. Simply use your imagination and an inspired blend of your favorite seasonal ingredients.

• Cheese, ham or bacon, spinach, tomato, and avocado are among the most popular choices. Pair any two for a winning combination.

• Leftover vegetable side dishes add savory complexity to omelets. Try spicy braised eggplant (page 207), grilled asparagus (page 184), or caramelized Brussels sprouts for distinctive flavor—especially when partnered with a good cheese.

In a small bowl, whisk together the eggs and a pinch of salt. Set a 7-inch (18-cm) nonstick frying pan over medium heat. Add 1 tablespoon butter to the pan, tilting the pan to distribute the butter evenly over the pan bottom. Pour half of the eggs into the pan. As the eggs begin to set along the edge, use a spatula to push the edges toward the centers, tilting the pan to let the raw egg flow to the pan edge, until the bottom is set but the top is still liquid, about 1 minute. Top half of the omelet with a filling of choice, fold the uncovered side of the omelet over the filling, and keep warm while you make the remaining omelet. Serve hot.

Onion & Herb Breakfast Potatoes

Nearly everybody likes home fries for breakfast, but this onion-laced potato sauté is just as satisfying and a lot tastier. Serve it alongside a hearty omelet or your favorite rendition of morning eggs.

SERVES 6–8

6 small Yukon gold potatoes

6 fingerling potatoes

6 small red potatoes

10 green onions, including tender green tops, cut into ½-inch (12-mm) lengths

1 Tbsp chopped fresh savory, or 1 tsp dried savory

5 Tbsp (2½ oz/75 g) butter

¼ cup (2 fl oz/60 ml) vegetable oil, plus more as needed

Salt and freshly ground pepper

¼ cup (½ oz/15 g) chopped fresh flat-leaf parsley

Fill a large bowl with cold water. Peel the Yukon gold potatoes, slice ⅛ inch (3 mm) thick, and immediately add to the water. Slice the unpeeled fingerling and red potatoes the same thickness and add to the water. At this point, the potatoes can stay in the water for up to 4 hours before cooking. Drain and pat dry with paper towels just before frying.

In a bowl, toss the green onions with the savory. In a large cast-iron frying pan over high heat, melt the butter with the oil. When the foam subsides, add the potatoes and onion mixture in alternating batches, season with salt and pepper, and allow an even brown crust to form on the bottom, 8–10 minutes. If necessary, add more oil and adjust the heat to prevent burning. Using a metal spatula, turn the mixture over, shaking the pan to redistribute. Continue cooking until browned on the bottom, about 5 minutes. Reduce the heat to medium-low, cover, and cook until the potatoes are almost tender, about 10 minutes. Uncover, raise the heat to medium-high, and carefully turn often until the potatoes are cooked through, about 5 minutes longer. Season with salt and pepper, sprinkle with parsley, and serve.

a modern classic

Sweet potatoes add more than their inimitable flavor to this updated morning standard. Served in place of the traditional russet potatoes, they deliver more vitamin A and C, fewer calories and carbs, and more fiber than regular spuds.

Sweet Potato Hash with Poached Eggs

Here is a great cool-weather breakfast, and it is easy to share the labor. You can work together on preparing the ingredients for cooking, and then one of you can cook the hash while the other one poaches the eggs. To make the dish vegetarian, omit the ham.

SERVES 6

2 orange-fleshed sweet potatoes, about ¾ lb (375 g) total weight, peeled and cut into slices ¾ inch (2 cm) thick

4 tsp grapeseed or canola oil

1 cup (5 oz/155 g) finely chopped red onion

½ Granny Smith apple, cored and diced

3 oz (90 g) Black Forest ham, diced

2 tsp fresh thyme leaves

¼ tsp sweet paprika

1 Tbsp distilled white vinegar

1 tsp salt

6 large eggs

Snipped fresh chives and fresh thyme leaves for garnish (optional)

In a large saucepan fitted with a steamer basket, bring 1 inch (2.5 cm) water to a boil. Evenly spread the sweet potato slices in the steamer basket, cover, and steam until they are tender but still offer some resistance when pierced gently with a fork, about 8 minutes. Remove the steamer basket and let the potatoes cool to room temperature. At this point, the potatoes can be tightly covered and refrigerated for up to 24 hours.

In a nonstick frying pan, heat 2 teaspoons of the oil over medium-high heat. Add the onion and apple and sauté until the onion is lightly browned, about 10 minutes. Cut the sweet potatoes into rough cubes and add them to the pan with the ham, thyme, and paprika. Continue to cook, stirring frequently, until the hash ingredients are browned and warmed through, 5–10 minutes.

While the hash is cooking, fill a deep sauté pan halfway with cold water. Add the vinegar and salt and place the pan over medium heat. When the water begins to simmer, break the eggs, one at a time, into a cup and slip each one gently into the water. Cook for 1 minute, then gently slide a spatula under the eggs to prevent them from sticking. Poach to the desired doneness, 3–5 minutes.

Divide the hash among individual plates. Using a slotted spoon, scoop the eggs from the simmering water, drain slightly, and place each on top of a serving of hash. Sprinkle chives and thyme over each serving, if desired, and serve right away.

CHAPTER TWO

STARTERS & SNACKS

All of me
loves
all of you

Tomato & Feta Tart

You do not need to be a seasoned baker to make this summertime tart. Store-bought, all-butter puff pastry dough is the secret to the golden brown, flaky crust. The last-minute sprinkling of fresh herbs is a must. Use the ones listed here, or your own flavor-enhancing favorites.

SERVES 4–6

1 sheet frozen puff pastry, about 9 oz (280 g), thawed according to package directions

All-purpose flour for dusting

1 cup (6 oz/185 g) cherry tomatoes, halved

8 ripe tomatoes, thinly sliced

6 oz (185 g) feta cheese, crumbled

1 Tbsp chopped fresh oregano

Salt and freshly ground pepper

6 sprigs fresh thyme

Preheat the oven to 400°F (200°C). Line a rimmed baking sheet with parchment paper.

Unfold the pastry sheet on a lightly floured work surface. Roll out into a 9-by-13-inch (23-by-33-cm) rectangle about ⅛ inch (3 mm) thick. Transfer the rectangle to the prepared baking sheet. Using a fork, prick the rectangle evenly all over. To create a border on the tart, fold over ½ inch (12 mm) of the pastry all the way around the edge.

Arrange the cherry tomato halves, sliced tomatoes, and cheese evenly on top of the pastry. Sprinkle evenly with the oregano, season with salt and pepper, and top with the thyme sprigs.

Bake until the pastry is puffed and golden brown, about 20 minutes. Remove from the oven and transfer to a work surface. Cut the tart into pieces and serve.

MODERN
HEIRLOOM

cook in season

Add an array of the best, fresh
heirloom tomatoes you can find and
this simple tart becomes something
truly special. Include a range of
sizes and colors for the best results.
A sprinkling of fresh herbs adds a
final grace note to this sublime tart.

Cheddar & Parmesan Cheese Straws

Cheese straws are easy to make, delicious to eat, and a welcome alternative to the usual cheese and crackers. Stand them upright in Picardie or other clear-glass tumblers, then nibble them alongside a freshly shaken cocktail (page 86) or other ice-cold drink.

MAKES ABOUT 30 STRAWS; SERVES 12–14

½ lb (250 g) sharp Cheddar cheese, shredded

2 oz (60 g) Parmesan cheese, grated

½ cup (4 oz/125 g) unsalted butter, at room temperature

½ tsp freshly ground white pepper

¼ tsp cayenne pepper

1 cup (5 oz/155 g) all-purpose flour, plus more for dusting

¼ cup (1 oz/30 g) topping of choice such as sesame seeds, poppy seeds, and/or sea salt

In a food processor, combine the cheeses, butter, white pepper, and cayenne and process to a smooth paste. Slowly add the flour, pulsing to blend. When all of the flour is incorporated, gather the dough into a ball. Wrap in plastic wrap and refrigerate for at least 1 hour and up to 3 hours.

Preheat the oven to 350°F (180°C). Lightly grease a baking sheet with butter or line it with parchment paper.

Remove the chilled dough from the refrigerator and cut into 7 equal pieces. On a lightly floured work surface, use your palm to roll each piece into a rope about the diameter of a drinking straw. Cut each rope into pieces 6–8 inches (15–20 cm) long.

Sprinkle the topping evenly on a sheet of aluminum foil. Roll each straw in the topping, coating lightly on all sides. Place the straws about 1 inch (2.5 cm) apart on the prepared baking sheet.

Bake until golden brown and lightly crisp, 15–20 minutes. Transfer the baking sheet to a wire rack and let cool for 5–10 minutes. Transfer the cheese straws to a platter and serve warm, or let cool completely and store in an airtight container at room temperature for up to 8 hours.

Figs with Caramelized Walnuts & Burrata

Marrying caramelized walnuts and creamy cheese with summer figs is an irresistible partnership. Figs are best in late summer. Select plump fruits that are soft to the touch but neither mushy nor bruised, and eat them as soon as possible after purchase.

SERVES 4–6

½ cup (2 oz/60 g) walnut halves

1 Tbsp honey

Pinch of salt

1 pint (about 12 oz/375 g) ripe figs, washed and halved lengthwise

1 ball burrata cheese, about 10 oz (315 g)

Mild crackers such as Carr's Whole Wheat

Preheat the oven to 350°F (180°C).

Arrange the nuts in a single layer on a baking sheet. Toast until golden brown, about 8–10 minutes.

In a small skillet, combine the honey and salt with 1 tablespoon water and bring to a boil. Add the nuts and reduce the heat to medium-low. Cook, stirring constantly, until the liquid evaporates, about 2 minutes. Transfer the nuts to a plate to cool. When cool, break apart any nuts that have stuck together.

Gently smash the fig halves on a cutting board. Arrange the figs, cheese, walnuts, and crackers on a platter. To serve, top a cracker with a swipe of cheese, a smashed fig half, and a caramelized walnut.

Snacks to Share

Marinated Olives

½ cup (2½ oz/75 g) *each* Picholine, Moroccan and Niçoise olives • 1 orange • 1 lemon • Leaves from 2 sprigs fresh thyme 1 clove garlic, minced • 1½ Tbsp extra-virgin olive oil

Rinse the olives under cold running water to remove any brine. Pat dry with paper towels. Using a citrus zester, remove half of the zest from the orange and the lemon in long strips. In a bowl, toss the olives with the citrus zests, thyme, garlic, and olive oil.

Just before serving, gently warm the olive mixture in a sauté pan over low heat to bring out the flavors. Serve with a small dish alongside for discarded pits.

MAKES ABOUT 1½ CUPS (7½ OZ/235 G)

Muhammara

3 large red bell peppers, roasted, peeled, and seeded or 1 jar (8 oz/250 g) roasted peppers • 1 cup (4 oz/125 g) walnuts, toasted • ⅔ cup (2½ oz/75 g) fine dried bread crumbs • 1 small yellow onion, chopped • 1 jalapeño or other hot chile, coarsely chopped, or 1 tablespoon red pepper flakes • 2 cloves garlic, finely chopped • 2 Tbsp *each* pomegranate molasses and extra-virgin olive oil • 1 Tbsp fresh lemon juice • 1 tsp ground cumin • Salt • 8–10 fresh mint leaves, torn

In a food processor or blender, combine the peppers, walnuts, bread crumbs, onion, chile, garlic, molasses, olive oil, lemon juice, cumin, and a pinch of salt and process just until combined and a coarse texture. Taste and adjust the seasoning, transfer to a bowl, stir in the mint, and serve.

MAKES ABOUT 2½ CUPS (1¼ LB/625 G)

Whether you've hit the waning end of a long day, feel a pang of mid-afternoon hunger, or just want to share a pre-dinner bite, a creamy dip or handful of nuts or olives is quick to satisfy.

Herb Aioli

1 clove garlic • 1 large egg • 1 tsp Dijon mustard • Zest and juice of 1 lemon • ½ cup (4 fl oz/125 ml) extra-virgin olive oil 2 Tbsp *each* fresh dill leaves and fresh flat-leaf parsley leaves, plus extra for garnish • Salt and freshly ground pepper

In a food processor, combine the garlic, egg, mustard, and lemon zest and juice and pulse a few times to blend. With the motor running, add the olive oil in a slow, steady stream and process until the aioli is emulsified, stopping to scrape down the sides of the bowl as needed. Add the dill and parsley and pulse until combined. Season with salt and pepper. Serve with a sprinkling of fresh chopped herbs over the top.

MAKES ABOUT 1 CUP (8 OZ/250 G)

Bacon-Glazed Spiced Nuts

2 cups (10 oz/315 g) mixed raw nuts • 1 large egg white, beaten slightly • 2 Tbsp granulated sugar • 1 Tbsp sea salt ½ tsp ground cumin • ¼ tsp *each* ground cinnamon, cayenne pepper, and ground ginger • ¼ lb (4 oz/125 g) sliced bacon

Preheat the oven to 350°F (180°C). Line a rimmed baking sheet with parchment paper.

In a bowl, combine the nuts and egg white; toss to coat. In another bowl, mix the sugar, salt, cumin, cinnamon, cayenne, and ginger. Add the spices to the nuts; toss to coat. Transfer to the prepared baking sheet. Bake, stirring often to break up any clumps, until lightly toasted, 15–20 minutes. Place on a plate and arrange in a single layer.

In a frying pan over medium heat, cook the bacon. Let cool on paper towels, then crumble over the nuts. Toss to mix.

MAKES ABOUT 2¼ CUPS (12 OZ/375 G)

Crispy Potato & Zucchini Haystack

If a spiralizer, a countertop tool that magically transforms solid vegetables into long, uniform noodle-like strands, was not among your wedding gifts, you'll want one for this and more. To save time, skip the homemade aioli and season 1 cup (8 fl oz/250 ml) store-bought mayonnaise with lemon zest and herbs.

SERVES 4

Herb Aioli (page 75)

Canola oil for frying

1 russet potato, peeled and ends trimmed

1 sweet potato, peeled and ends trimmed

1 zucchini, ends trimmed

Kosher salt

Make the herb aioli. Cover and refrigerate until ready to serve.

In a wide, deep, heavy pot or Dutch oven over medium-high heat, fill two-thirds full with canola oil and heat to 350°F (180°C) on a deep-frying thermometer. Line a plate with paper towels.

Meanwhile, spiralize the russet potato, sweet potato, and zucchini using the fine shredder blade, stopping to cut the strands every 3–4 rotations. Spread out the vegetables on a baking sheet and pat dry with paper towels.

Working in batches, deep-fry the russet potato, stirring occasionally with a skimmer or slotted spoon, until crispy and golden brown, 4–6 minutes per batch. Using the skimmer, transfer to the prepared plate and season with salt. Repeat to fry the sweet potato and zucchini. Stack the potatoes and zucchini on a serving platter. Serve right away with the aioli.

zucchini

russet
potato

sweet
potato

herb
aioli

artisan
bread

pancetta

pea
shoots

nectarine

fig

gorgonzola

thyme

honeycomb

cherry
tomato

walnuts

Quick Toast Five Ways

At the end of a long day, or in the middle of a lazy one, a quick and easy toast is all that's needed for a quick hit of nourishment. Choose your bread variety with both care and abandon—first consider the topping of choice, then enhance it with slices cut from unique, artisanal loaves.

quick toasts

8 slices good-quality bread
4 tablespoons butter

Toast the bread until golden at the edges. Spread evenly with butter. Spoon topping of choice evenly over each toast.

SERVES 4–8

fava bean
+
goat cheese
+
mint

½ lb (8 oz/250 g) fava beans, outer pods removed
5 oz (140 g) fresh goat cheese
2 Tbsp chopped fresh mint, plus small leaves for garnish
2 Tbsp extra-virgin olive oil
Salt and ground pepper

Blanch fava beans in boiling salted water for 1 minute. Drain, plunge in ice water, and drain again. Using your fingers, remove the skins. Set aside. Blend goat cheese with chopped fresh mint and chives. Spread the herbed cheese on toasts and sprinkle a few blanched fresh fava beans on top. Drizzle with extra-virgin olive oil, season with salt and pepper, and garnish with fresh mint leaves.

goat cheese
+
walnuts

6 oz (180 g) fresh goat cheese
¼ cup (1 oz/30 g) chopped walnuts
1 tsp walnut oil
Salt and cracked pepper
Honey for drizzling
½ teaspoon fresh thyme leaves

Spread the goat cheese on slices of lightly toasted whole-grain bread, sprinkle with the walnuts, and drizzle with the walnut oil. Bake in a 375°F(190°C) oven until warmed, 5 minutes. Remove from the oven. Season with salt and pepper, drizzle with honey, and sprinkle with thyme.

prosciutto
+
nectarine

4 nectarines, halved and pitted
½ lb (8 oz/225 g) prosciutto, thinly sliced
2 Tbsp extra-virgin olive oil
Sea salt and ground pepper

Using a mandoline, shave thin slices from the nectarines. Place alternating folded slices of nectarine and prosciutto on toasted baguette or ciabatta slices. Drizzle with olive oil and season with salt and pepper.

avocado
+
cherry tomato

2 avocados, peeled and pitted
Fresh lemon juice from ½ lemon
1 pint (12 oz/340 g) yellow and red cherry tomatoes, halved
4 sprigs fresh basil
4 Tbsp extra-virgin olive oil
Salt and ground pepper

Mash avocado with lemon juice until spreadable but chunky and spread on toasted ciabatta or pugliese slices. Top with the tomatoes and fresh basil leaves. Drizzle with olive oil and season with salt and pepper.

gorgonzola
+
fig

8 oz (250 g) Gorgonzola cheese
8 fresh figs, thinly sliced
½ cup (½ oz/15 g) baby arugula leaves
2 Tbsp extra-virgin olive oil
Sea salt and ground pepper

Spread gorgonzola on toasted baguette or walnut bread slices. Top with a few thin slices of fresh fig and some arugula leaves. Drizzle with olive oil and season with salt and pepper.

Fresh Vegetable Spring Rolls

These light, healthy spring rolls are perfect finger food on warm days. Rolling the rice paper takes a bit of practice, so you will both want to give it try. Loosely wrap any leftover rolls in damp paper towels and store them in an airtight container in the refrigerator for up to 1 day.

MAKES 12 ROLLS; SERVES 4

½ lb (8 oz/250 g) shiitake mushrooms

2 tsp canola or peanut oil

1 clove garlic, pressed or minced

1 tsp soy sauce, preferably low-sodium

7 oz (220 g) thin dried rice noodles

12 rice paper wrappers,
8½ inches (21.5 cm) in diameter

2 red bell peppers, seeded and thinly sliced

2 ripe avocados, pitted, peeled, and sliced

2 carrots, peeled and cut into matchsticks

1 cup (1 oz/30 g) firmly packed mixed fresh herb sprigs such as mint, cilantro, and basil

Trim the stems from the mushrooms and discard or reserve for soup or stock. Slice the caps and set aside.

In a large nonstick frying pan over medium-high heat, warm 1½ teaspoons of the oil. Add the garlic and cook, stirring, until fragrant but not browned, about 30 seconds. Add the mushroom caps and sauté until they release their liquid, 3–4 minutes. Add the soy sauce and cook until the pan is dry, about 1 minute. Transfer to a bowl and set aside.

Bring a pot of water to a boil over high heat. Add the noodles, stir to separate, and cook until tender, 3–5 minutes or according to the package directions. Drain in a colander and rinse under cold running water. Wipe the pot dry, return the noodles to the pot, and toss with the remaining ½ teaspoon oil.

Fill a large, shallow bowl with very hot tap water. Soak 1 rice paper wrapper at a time until just flexible, 10–15 seconds. Shake off any excess water and lay the wrapper flat on a work surface. Across the lower half of the wrapper, place rows of noodles, mushrooms, bell pepper, avocado, carrots, and herbs. Fold the edge closest to you over the filling, fold in the sides, then roll up tightly. Repeat to make the remaining rolls. Cut each roll in half on the diagonal and serve.

chile dipping sauce

To make a quick sauce for these homemade rolls, mix ¼ cup (2 oz/60 g) *each* of sugar and fresh lime juice with 5 tablespoons Asian fish sauce, 1 clove minced garlic, ½ teaspoon dried chile flakes, and ½ cup (4 fl oz/125 ml) water.

Crab Cakes with Lemon Aioli

You can eat half of these crab-packed cakes and save the remainder for a quick starter on another evening. Serve them as is, or nestle them atop a bed of lightly dressed tender greens such as watercress, mâche, or baby arugula.

MAKES 8 CAKES; SERVES 4

FOR THE LEMON AIOLI

1 cup (8 fl oz/250 ml) mayonnaise

Grated zest of 1 lemon

2 Tbsp fresh lemon juice

1 clove garlic, minced

Sea salt and freshly ground pepper

FOR THE CRAB CAKES

¾ cup (4 oz/125 g) panko bread crumbs

1 large egg, beaten

1 Tbsp Dijon mustard

2 tsp Worcestershire sauce

¼ tsp hot-pepper sauce

1 Tbsp chopped fresh flat-leaf parsley

1 lb (500 g) lump crabmeat, picked over for shells and cartilage

Canola oil for frying

Lemon wedges for serving

To make the lemon aioli, in a small bowl, mix together the mayonnaise, lemon zest and juice, and garlic. Season with salt and pepper. Reserve ¼ cup (2 fl oz/60 ml) of the aioli; cover and refrigerate the remainder until serving.

Line a rimmed baking sheet with parchment paper. To make the crab cakes, in a bowl, mix together ¼ cup (⅓ oz/10 g) of the bread crumbs, the reserved aioli, the egg, mustard, Worcestershire sauce, hot-pepper sauce, and parsley. Add the crabmeat and mix gently until combined. Divide the mixture into 8 equal portions and shape each portion into a thick cake. Spread the remaining ½ cup bread crumbs in a shallow dish. Coat the cakes evenly with the bread crumbs and transfer to the prepared baking sheet. Refrigerate for 15 minutes.

In a large frying pan over medium-high heat, warm a thin film of oil until it shimmers. Working in batches to avoid crowding, gently add the crab cakes and cook until the undersides are golden brown, about 2½ minutes. Carefully flip the cakes and cook until golden brown on the second sides, about 2½ minutes longer. Using a slotted spatula, transfer to paper towels to drain briefly. Repeat with the remaining cakes, adding oil to the pan as needed.

Serve the crab cakes right away, with the lemon wedges and the extra lemon aioli on the side.

Spicy Shrimp with Herb Dipping Sauce

Here is a divinely simple dish that calls for seeking out the very best shrimp available. With that task done, the rest of the recipe is easy and quick. Serve with glasses of chilled champagne or some frothy mugs of beer to temper the shrimp's spicy heat.

SERVES 6–8

FOR THE HERB DIPPING SAUCE

⅓ cup (½ oz/15 g) firmly packed fresh basil leaves

1 green onion, coarsely chopped

2 Tbsp fresh flat-leaf parsley leaves

2 Tbsp capers

1 Tbsp fresh oregano leaves

1 Tbsp fresh lemon juice

2 tsp Dijon mustard

1 clove garlic, coarsely chopped

3 Tbsp extra-virgin olive oil

1 tsp mixed peppercorns

2 lb (1 kg) shrimp in the shell

Generous pinch of red pepper flakes

Sea salt

2 Tbsp vegetable oil

4 cloves garlic, minced

Lemon wedges for serving

To make the herb dipping sauce, in a food processor, combine the basil, green onion, parsley, capers, oregano, lemon juice, mustard, and garlic and process until finely chopped. With the processor running, slowly pour in the olive oil and process until the mixture forms a chunky purée. (The sauce can be covered and refrigerated for up to 3 days.)

Using a mortar and pestle, finely crush the peppercorns. In a bowl, combine the shrimp, half of the crushed peppercorns, the red pepper flakes, and 1 teaspoon salt and toss together. Set aside.

In a wok over high heat, warm the vegetable oil. Add the garlic, remaining crushed peppercorns, and 1 teaspoon salt and cook, stirring, for 1 minute. Add the shrimp and cook until opaque throughout, 3–4 minutes. Transfer to a platter and serve hot with lemon wedges and the dipping sauce. Serve with a small bowl or plate for discarded shells.

CELEBRATE HOME

A WARM WELCOME FOR FAMILY & FRIENDS

Summer weekends made festive with handcrafted
cocktails, winter get-togethers brightened with
an array of savory small plates—your newlywed status
brings with it countless occasions for entertaining.
In these pages are a wealth of fresh and easy ideas to help
you create special moments as you welcome family and
friends to your home. Look to your local farmers' market
for inspiration on offering drinks and appetizers
that make the most of seasonal flavors.

Shaken Cocktails For Two

Most cocktail shakers hold the ideal amount for a pair of drinks— quite convenient for the newly wed! The clattering of a cocktail shaker signals celebration—and in this case, it's for two.

Salty Dog

Kosher salt • 1 grapefruit wedge plus 2 slices for garnish • Ice • 4 fl oz (125 ml) vodka or gin • 6 fl oz (180 ml) grapefruit juice

Pour salt onto a plate. Moisten the rims of 2 old-fashioned glasses with the grapefruit wedge. Gently dip the rims of the glasses into the salt to coat lightly. Set the prepared glasses aside.

Fill a cocktail shaker a third full with ice. Add the vodka and grapefruit juice. Cover, shake vigorously, and strain into the salt-rimmed glasses. Drop a grapefruit slice into each glass and serve.

Manhattan

Ice • 5 fl oz (140 ml) bourbon or rye whiskey 1½ fl oz (15 ml) sweet vermouth • 4 dashes Angostura bitters • 2 olives

Fill a cocktail shaker a third full with ice. Add the whiskey, vermouth, and bitters. Cover, shake vigorously, and strain into 2 chilled Manhattan glasses. Garnish with the olives and serve.

Jalapeño Margarita

1 Tbsp kosher salt mixed with a generous pinch of paprika • 1 lime wedge • ¼–½ small jalapeño pepper, sliced • 3 fl oz (45 ml) tequila • 2 fl oz (30 ml) fresh lime juice 1 fl oz (15 ml) Grand Marnier • 2 Tbsp simple syrup or orange juice • Ice

Pour the salt mixture onto a plate. Moisten the rims of 2 margarita glasses with the lime wedge. Gently dip the rims of the glasses into the salt to coat lightly. Set the prepared glasses aside.

Reserve some chile slices for garnish. In a cocktail shaker, gently muddle the remaining chile with the tequila. Add the lime juice, Grand Marnier, and simple syrup. Fill the shaker a third full with ice. Cover, and shake vigorously. Strain into the prepared glasses. Drop a few slices of chile into each glass and serve.

Orange Blossom Gin Fizz

Ice • 3 fl oz (90 ml) gin • 1½ fl oz (45 ml) yuzu or fresh lemon juice • ¼ orange, cut into 2 wedges • ¾ tsp orange flower water 1 oz (30 ml) simple syrup • Club soda Orange blossoms for garnish (optional)

Fill a cocktail shaker a third full with ice. Add gin, yuzu juice, orange wedges, orange flower water, and simple syrup. Cover, shake vigorously, and strain into 2 small highball glasses filled with ice. Top with club soda. Garnish with orange blossoms (if using) and serve.

Jack Rose

Ice • 4 fl oz (125 ml) applejack or other apple brandy • 1½ fl oz (45 ml) grenadine 2 fl oz (60 ml) fresh lime juice • 2 thin apple slices

Fill a cocktail shaker a third full with ice. Add the applejack, grenadine, and lime juice and shake vigorously. Strain into 2 chilled martini glasses, garnish with the apple slices, and serve.

CHAPTER THREE

SOUPS & SALADS

You stole my heart, but I'll let you keep it

Pork Ramen
with Bean Sprouts

Asian markets and well-stocked grocery stores carry fresh ramen noodles, but you can also use dried ramen. Substitute cilantro and fresh mint for Thai basil, if you wish. Find shichimi togarashi, *a traditional addition to ramen, in specialty supermarkets.*

SERVES 4

FOR THE MARINADE

8 cloves garlic, finely chopped

1-inch (2.5-cm) piece fresh ginger, peeled and finely chopped

¼ cup (2 fl oz/60 ml) soy sauce, preferably low-sodium

¼ cup (2 fl oz/60 ml) rice wine

1 Tbsp firmly packed dark brown sugar

1 tsp freshly ground black pepper

1 tsp ground white pepper

½ tsp cayenne pepper

2 Tbsp Asian sesame oil

1 pork tenderloin (1½–1¾ lb/750–875 g)

2 tomatoes, halved horizontally (optional)

Canola oil for brushing

Salt and freshly ground black pepper

4 cups (32 fl oz/1 l) chicken broth

1 Tbsp Asian fish sauce

1 lb (500 g) fresh ramen noodles

2 cups (8 oz/250 g) fresh bean sprouts for garnish

Fresh Thai basil sprigs for garnish

4 hard-boiled eggs (page 248), halved or sliced, for garnish

Shichimi togarashi for garnish (see note above)

To make the marinade, in a large resealable plastic bag combine the garlic, ginger, soy sauce, rice wine, brown sugar, black pepper, white pepper, and cayenne. Massage the bag to dissolve the sugar, then add the sesame oil. Spoon out 3 tablespoons of the marinade into a soup pot or large saucepan and set aside for the broth.

Add the pork tenderloin to the bag with the marinade, turning to coat. Seal the bag and refrigerate for at least 3 hours or up to 6 hours.

Preheat the oven to 425°F (220°C). If using tomatoes, arrange them on a rimmed baking sheet, brush with oil, and season with salt and pepper. Bake until the tomatoes are tender but hold their shape, about 20 minutes. Set aside. Do not turn off the oven.

Add the chicken broth and fish sauce to the marinade in the pot. Cover partially and bring to a simmer over low heat.

Pat the pork dry with paper towels and discard the marinade. Brush the pork with the oil and place on a rack in a small roasting pan. Cook until the pork is nicely browned on the outside, barely pink in the center, and registers 155°F (68°C) on an instant-read thermometer inserted into the thickest part, 15–20 minutes. Place the pork on a cutting board and let rest for 5–10 minutes.

Meanwhile, cook the noodles according to the package directions. Drain the noodles and rinse under cold running water. Divide among 4 wide, shallow bowls.

Cut the pork on the diagonal into thin slices. Taste and season the broth mixture. Divide the broth among the bowls. Add a few slices of pork, a tomato half (if using), bean sprouts, basil sprigs, and an egg to each bowl and serve. Pass a small bowl of *shichimi togarashi* at the table.

For millions around the world, a well-executed ramen bowl is comfort food like no other. With its mix of textures and flavors, it is universally appealing—especially when cooks experiment with their own favorite additions.

Roasted Tomato & Sweet Onion Soup with Torn Croutons

The farmers' market is the best place to find the firm, flavorful tomatoes and the sweet onion that will make the difference between a good soup and a great one. Store leftover soup in the refrigerator for up to 3 days; reheat gently.

SERVES 4–6

3 lb (1.5 kg) ripe tomatoes

2 Tbsp olive oil

2 Tbsp balsamic vinegar

1 clove garlic, minced

2 tsp fresh thyme leaves

Salt and freshly ground pepper

1 sweet onion, chopped

½ cup (4 fl oz/125 ml) dry white wine

3 cups (24 fl oz/750 ml) low-sodium chicken broth

½ cup (1 oz/30 g) torn croutons (page 248)

Preheat the oven to 325°F (165°C). Halve the tomatoes and place, cut side up, on a baking sheet. In a small bowl, whisk together 1 tablespoon of the olive oil, the vinegar, garlic, thyme, ¼ teaspoon salt, and ¼ teaspoon pepper. Spoon the mixture evenly over the tomatoes. Bake until the tomatoes are soft and wrinkled, about 1 hour.

In a soup pot over medium-high heat, warm the remaining 1 tablespoon olive oil. Add the onion and cook, stirring often and reducing the heat as needed to prevent scorching, until soft, 5–7 minutes. Add the wine, raise the heat to medium-high, and bring to a boil. Cook until the liquid is evaporated, 2–3 minutes. Stir in the chicken broth and tomatoes, using a wooden spoon to scrape up any browned bits from the bottom of the pan, and return to a boil. Reduce the heat to medium-low, cover, and simmer for 10 minutes to allow the flavors to blend.

In a blender or food processor, working in batches if necessary, process the soup until smooth. (Alternatively, pass the soup through a food mill.) Return to the pot and season with salt and pepper. Reheat the soup gently over medium heat just until hot. Ladle into warmed individual bowls, garnish with the croutons, and serve right away.

Ginger-Carrot Soup with Roasted Cauliflower Crumbs

Ginger, coriander, and fennel give this silky purée warm Indian flavors. The best carrots to use are the big, fat type favored for juicing. On a busy weekday night, pair the soup with your choice of Quick Toasts (page 79) for an easy supper.

SERVES 4

1 large cauliflower, trimmed

2 Tbsp coconut oil

1¼ lb (625 g) large carrots, peeled and thinly sliced

1 large yellow onion, diced

1 clove garlic, chopped

1-inch (2.5-cm) piece fresh ginger, peeled and chopped

2½ tsp ground coriander

½ tsp ground fennel seeds

¾ cup (6 fl oz/180 ml) unsweetened coconut milk

Salt and freshly ground pepper

Preheat the oven to 425°F (220°C).

Cut the cauliflower into ¼-inch (6-mm) pieces, trimming and discarding most of the stem; you should have about 2 cups (4 oz/120 g) tiny florets. Place the cauliflower on a rimmed baking sheet, drizzle with 1 tablespoon of the oil, and toss until the florets are evenly coated. Bake the cauliflower for 15 minutes, stir, and continue baking until the florets are well browned and crisped in places, 5–10 minutes longer. Set aside.

While the cauliflower roasts, in a large saucepan over medium-high heat, warm the remaining 1 tablespoon oil. Add the carrots, onion, garlic, and ginger and sauté until the onion is lightly colored, about 5 minutes. Add the coriander and fennel and cook, stirring constantly, until the spices are fragrant, about 30 seconds. Remove from the heat and let cool for 10 minutes. In a blender or food processor, process the soup until smooth. Blend in the coconut milk. Return the soup to the saucepan over medium heat and reheat, stirring occasionally to prevent scorching. Season to taste with salt and pepper.

Ladle the soup into bowls. Garnish with the roasted cauliflower crumbs and serve.

weeknight bowl

These flavorful bowls can be on the table within an easy 20 minutes. Make them as light or hearty as you wish—extra fresh ingredients can be added (or not) just before eating.

Chicken, Tortilla & Lime Soup

If you have leftover home-roasted or store-bought rotisserie chicken on hand, this soup is the ideal solution for a weeknight dinner after a long workday. The soup is delicious as is, but you can make it heartier by stirring in some corn and/or peeled, seeded, and diced tomatoes with the chicken.

SERVES 4–6

1 Tbsp olive oil

½ white onion, finely chopped

½ small jalapeño chile, seeded, deribbed, and minced

6 cups (48 fl oz/1.5 l) chicken broth

2 cups (12 oz/375 g) cooked, shredded chicken

Juice of 3–4 limes

Salt

1½ cups (4½ oz/140 g) corn tortilla chips, broken into pieces

½ cup (2½ oz/75 g) crumbled queso fresco

1 avocado, pitted, peeled, and diced

¼ cup (⅓ oz/10 g) chopped fresh cilantro

4 radishes, thinly sliced

In a large saucepan over medium-high heat, warm the olive oil. Add the onion and sauté until translucent, about 3 minutes. Add the jalapeño and stir until fragrant, about 1 minute. Pour in the broth and bring to a boil. Add the shredded chicken, reduce the heat to medium, and simmer until the chicken is heated through, about 3 minutes. Add the lime juice and salt to taste.

Ladle into bowls. Garnish with the tortilla chips, queso fresco, avocado, cilantro, and radishes, and serve.

French Onion Soup

Meltingly tender onions, a robust stock, and cheese-laden croutons—these are the indispensable elements that make this soup a hallmark of French cuisine and a favorite of American tables. A kitchen torch is a good alternative to the broiler for melting the cheese with ease.

SERVES 8

2 Tbsp unsalted butter

2½ lb (1.25 kg) yellow onions, halved and thinly sliced

1 Tbsp all-purpose flour

1 cup (8 fl oz/250 ml) dry white wine

8 cups (64 fl oz/2 l) beef stock

2 tsp minced fresh thyme or 1 tsp dried thyme

1 bay leaf

Salt and freshly ground pepper

1 crusty baguette

2⅔ cups (10½ oz/330 g) shredded Gruyère cheese

In a large, heavy sauté pan over medium heat, melt the butter. Add the onions, stir well, cover, and cook for 5 minutes. Uncover, reduce the heat to medium-low, and cook, stirring occasionally, until tender and deep golden brown, about 30 minutes. Sprinkle the flour over the onions and stir until combined. Gradually stir in the wine and stock, then the thyme and bay leaf. Bring to a boil over high heat, reduce the heat to medium-low, and simmer, uncovered, until slightly reduced, about 30 minutes. Season with salt and pepper. Discard the bay leaf.

Meanwhile, preheat the broiler. Cut the baguette into 16 slices, sizing them so that 2 slices fit inside each of eight 12-ounce (375-ml) ovenproof soup crocks. Arrange the bread slices on a baking sheet and broil, turning once, until lightly toasted on both sides, about 1 minute total. Set the slices aside. Position the oven rack about 12 inches (30 cm) from the heat source and leave the broiler on.

Ladle the hot soup into the crocks. Place 2 toasted bread slices, overlapping if necessary, on top of the soup and sprinkle each crock evenly with about ⅓ cup (1½ oz/45 g) of the cheese. Broil until the cheese is bubbling, about 2 minutes. Serve right away.

Beef Pho

This simple yet satisfying noodle soup is comfort food, Southeast Asian–style. It combines a light-bodied broth and bright flavors that will warm you up on a cool night. Freezing the tenderloin for 1 hour makes it easier to cut into thin and even slices.

SERVES 4

6 oz (185 g) flat rice noodles

2 star anise pods

2 Tbsp coriander seeds

1 cinnamon stick

4 whole cloves

1 beef tenderloin, ½ lb (250 g), wrapped in plastic wrap and frozen for 1 hour

2 limes, cut into wedges

4 Tbsp fresh cilantro leaves

½ red onion, thinly sliced

2 small red chiles, seeded and thinly sliced

8 cups (64 fl oz/2 l) beef or chicken broth

4-inch (10-cm) piece fresh ginger, peeled and minced

2 Tbsp Asian fish sauce

2 tsp sugar

Sriracha chile sauce

In a bowl, combine the noodles with hot water to cover and let soak for 10 minutes. Drain.

In a small frying pan over medium heat, toast the star anise, coriander seeds, cinnamon, and cloves, stirring often, until fragrant, 2–3 minutes. Set aside.

Cut the beef diagonally into paper-thin slices. Cover with plastic wrap and refrigerate.

Arrange the limes, cilantro leaves, onion, and chiles on a platter. Cover with plastic wrap and refrigerate until serving.

In a large saucepan over medium-high heat, combine the broth, ginger, fish sauce, sugar, and toasted spices. Bring to a boil, reduce the heat to low, and simmer for 30 minutes. Strain the soup through a fine-mesh sieve, discarding the solids. Return the soup to the pan, bring to a boil, add the noodles, and cook for 5 minutes.

Using tongs, remove the noodles from the soup and divide equally among 4 warm bowls. Divide the reserved beef slices evenly among the bowls. Ladle the hot soup directly over the beef, adding enough to cover the noodles and cook the meat. Serve, passing the platter of lime wedges, cilantro, red onion, chiles, and Sriracha at the table.

PERFECT PARTNERSHIPS

PAIR SIMPLE DISHES FOR EASY EVENINGS

Cozy nights together can be wonderfully simple.
Start with a hearty homemade soup or stew, then
round out the menu by bringing home a loaf of artisanal
whole-grain bread or a crusty baguette from
a local bakery and a block of sweet cream butter
or a wedge of aged white Cheddar or other favorite cheese.
Add a bottle of your favorite wine and you might
just discover that your best date night is the
one you spend at home.

Tuscan Farro Soup with White Beans, Tomatoes & Basil

Hearty enough to be the main course, this soup marries a handful of classic Tuscan flavors. Look for semipearled (semiperlato) farro, which retains some of the bran and thus is better for you. Serve with a good Italian red, such as a Chianti or Sangiovese.

SERVES 6

½ cup (3 oz/90 g) farro

Salt and freshly ground pepper

3 Tbsp olive oil

1 large yellow onion, chopped

3 cloves garlic, minced

4 cups (32 fl oz/1 l) chicken broth

1 can (15 oz/470 g) cannellini beans, rinsed

1 can (14½ oz/455 g) diced tomatoes

2½ oz (75 g) baby spinach

½ cup (¾ oz/20 g) chopped fresh basil

In a small saucepan, bring 1½ cups (12 fl oz/375 ml) water to a boil. Add the farro and a pinch of salt, reduce the heat to low, and cook, partially covered, until all the water is absorbed, 20–25 minutes.

In a large, heavy pot over medium-high heat, warm the olive oil. Add the onion and garlic and sauté until very soft, about 5 minutes. Add the broth and bring to a boil. Reduce the heat to low and add the beans, tomatoes, and farro. Bring to a simmer and cook, uncovered, for 10 minutes. Add the spinach and basil and stir just until wilted. Season with salt and pepper. Ladle the soup into bowls and serve.

Baby Spinach Salad with Pickled Shallot & Pancetta

This salad makes a lovely side to hot soup in the cold-weather months. If you have no pancetta on hand but do have bacon, it makes a fine substitute. For an extra dose of protein, toss the spinach with a little crumbled fresh goat cheese.

SERVES 4

1 shallot, halved and thinly sliced

¼ cup (2 fl oz/60 ml) red wine vinegar

2 Tbsp sugar

¼ lb (125 g) pancetta, cut into ¼-inch (6-mm) dice

1 Tbsp extra-virgin olive oil

Salt and freshly ground pepper

8 oz (250 g) baby spinach

Put the shallot in a heatproof bowl. In a small saucepan over medium heat, combine the vinegar, sugar, and ¼ cup (2 fl oz/60 ml) water. Bring to a boil and simmer, stirring, until the sugar is dissolved. Pour the hot vinegar mixture over the shallot and let stand, uncovered at room temperature, for at least 30 minutes or up to 2 hours.

In a dry frying pan over medium heat, sauté the pancetta until crispy and the fat is rendered, about 10 minutes. Using a slotted spoon, transfer to paper towels to drain. Pour the hot fat into another heatproof bowl.

Strain the shallot, reserving the pickling liquid. Whisk ¼ cup (2 fl oz/60 ml) of the pickling liquid into the pancetta fat along with the olive oil, ½ teaspoon salt, and pepper to taste. Taste and adjust the seasoning with the pickling liquid, if needed.

Place the spinach in a large salad bowl and scatter the shallot over the top. Drizzle in the dressing and toss gently to coat. Sprinkle the pancetta on top and serve.

*meyer lemon
vinaigrette*

pomegranate

pea shoots

figs

watercress

asparagus

lettuce

*english
peas*

Seasonal Salads Four Ways

The best fresh produce of each season brings optimal flavor to inspired salad combinations. A few great ingredients and a simple vinaigrette are all that's required. Each tasty blend below makes enough to serve six.

basic vinaigrette

1 Tbsp white wine vinegar
or red wine vinegar

3–4 Tbsp extra-virgin olive oil

Salt and freshly ground pepper

In a jar, combine the vinegar with the olive oil and salt and pepper to taste. Cover and shake until well blended.

grapefruit vinaigrette

2 tsp *each* white wine vinegar and grapefruit juice

1 Tbsp *each* minced shallot and minced fresh chives

3–4 Tbsp extra-virgin olive oil

Salt and freshly ground pepper

In a jar, combine the vinegar, grapefruit juice, shallot, chives, olive oil, and salt and pepper to taste. Cover and shake until blended.

meyer lemon vinaigrette

Shredded zest and juice from 1 Meyer lemon

3–4 Tbsp extra-virgin olive oil

Salt and freshly ground pepper

Pinch of sugar (optional)

In a jar, combine the zest and juice with the olive oil and salt and pepper to taste. Cover and shake until well blended. Taste and adjust the sweetness with sugar, if needed.

pea shoots + asparagus

2 cups (10 oz/315 g) shelled fresh English peas

2 lb (1 kg) thin asparagus tips

2 cups (2 oz/60 g) pea shoots

Meyer Lemon Vinaigrette (at left)

Blanch the peas in boiling water for 1 minute. Refresh in ice water, then drain. Blanch the asparagus in boiling water for 2 minutes. Refresh in ice water, then drain. In a bowl, combine the peas, asparagus, and pea shoots. Toss with the Meyer lemon vinaigrette.

pomegranate + persimmon

2 heads frisée lettuce, leaves separated

½ cup (2 oz/60 g) toasted walnut halves

1 small pomegranate, seeded

1 Fuyu persimmon

1 red Bartlett pear

6 fresh figs

Basic Vinaigrette (at left) with red wine vinegar

In a large bowl, combine the frisée, walnuts, and pomegranate seeds. Core and thinly slice the persimmon and pear, cut the figs in half, and add the fruit to the frisée mixture. Toss with basic vinaigrette.

tomato + watermelon

1 mini seedless watermelon, about 4 lb (2 kg)

1¾ lb (875 g) heirloom tomatoes

2 Persian cucumbers, sliced

2 Tbsp *each* extra-virgin olive oil and white balsamic vinegar

3 oz (90 g) feta cheese, crumbled

½ cup (½ oz/15 g) fresh mint leaves

Cut the watermelon in half, cut off the rind, and cut the flesh into thin slices. Core and thinly slice the tomatoes. In a bowl, combine the watermelon, tomatoes, and cucumber slices. Drizzle with the olive oil and vinegar, then sprinkle with the feta and mint.

grapefruit + crab

2 cups (2 oz/60 g) watercress leaves

Grapefruit Vinaigrette (at left)

2 pink grapefruits, segmented

2 avocados, sliced

½ lb (250 g) fresh lump crabmeat

Place the watercress in a large bowl. Drizzle the vinaigrette over the top and toss to mix. Scatter the grapefruit, avocados, and crabmeat over the top, then toss gently to mix.

Mostly Herbs Salad with French Vinaigrette

Tender herbs and edible blossoms are the star ingredients in this colorful mix. Greens this fresh need little embellishment. Dress them with just a light coating of the vinaigrette. Cover and store any leftover dressing in the refrigerator for up to 5 days.

SERVES 4–6

FOR THE FRENCH VINAIGRETTE

2 Tbsp Champagne or white wine vinegar

2 tsp Dijon mustard

1 Tbsp fresh lemon juice

1 small shallot, finely diced

1 small garlic clove, minced

½ cup (4 fl oz/125 ml) extra-virgin olive oil

Salt and freshly ground pepper

6 handfuls mixed micro greens (mâche, lamb's lettuce, pea sprouts, or watercress)

1 cup (1 oz/30 g) mixed fresh herbs (flat-leaf parsley, basil, mint, chervil, or thyme leaves)

½ English cucumber

½ cup (½ oz/15 g) edible blossoms (see note, page 105)

½ cup (2 oz/60 g) toasted pumpkin seeds (pepitas)

To make the French vinaigrette, in a small jar or other covered container, combine the vinegar, mustard, lemon juice, shallot, and garlic. Cover and shake until well blended. Using a fork, mix in the olive oil until well blended and emulsified. Season to taste with salt and pepper. Set aside.

Wash the micro greens and gently pat dry on a cloth towel. For herbs with large leaves, such as basil and mint, cut or tear into ribbons. Peel the cucumber and, using a mandoline or vegetable peeler, shave lengthwise into thin ribbons.

In a large salad bowl, combine the greens, herbs, cucumber, blossoms, and pumpkin seeds. Cover with a clean towel and refrigerate until ready to dress.

Just before serving, drizzle with the dressing and toss gently to mix. Serve at once.

seasonal salad blooms

Fresh edible blossoms add both color and flavor to tender salad greens. Try herb blossoms such as those from thyme, basil, chives, and rosemary, or use flowers such as nasturtiums, marigolds, roses, and pansies.

Thai Grilled Beef & Herb Salad

In Thai cooking, the combination of grilled meats and an herb-centric collection of greens with a slightly salty dressing is a hallmark preparation. The low-fat vinaigrette and lean meat make this a healthy main-course salad. Substitute chicken for the steak, if you wish.

SERVES 4–8

FOR THE DRESSING

¼ cup (2 fl oz/60 ml) Asian sesame oil

2 cloves garlic, minced

1 tsp peeled and minced fresh ginger

2 Tbsp fresh lime juice

2 Tbsp Asian fish sauce or soy sauce

2 tsp honey

¾ tsp chile sauce such as sriracha

½ lb (250 g) skirt steak

1 Tbsp peanut or rice bran oil

1 romaine lettuce heart, cored and chopped (about 2 cups/4 oz/125 g)

½ cucumber

¼ red onion, very thinly sliced lengthwise

¼ cup (⅓ oz/10 g) loosely packed chopped fresh mint leaves

¼ cup (⅓ oz/10 g) loosely packed chopped fresh cilantro leaves

¼ cup (⅓ oz/10 g) loosely packed chopped fresh basil leaves

¼ cup (1¼ oz/40 g) chopped roasted peanuts

To make the dressing, in a small frying pan over medium heat, warm the sesame oil until shimmering. Remove from the heat and add the garlic and ginger. Whisk in the lime juice, fish sauce, honey, and chile sauce. Pour into a large bowl and set aside.

Prepare a charcoal or gas grill for direct grilling over high heat and oil the grill grate, or preheat a stove-top grill pan over high heat. Pat the steak dry, then rub it all over with the peanut oil. Place over the hottest part of the fire or in the grill pan and cook, turning once, until etched with grill marks on both sides, 5–10 minutes total for medium-rare or until done to your liking. Transfer to a carving board or a platter and let cool slightly.

When the steak is cool enough to handle, cut on the diagonal across the grain into strips about ½ inch (12 mm) wide, reserving the juices. Add the steak and its juices to the bowl with the dressing and toss to coat thoroughly. Cover and marinate at room temperature for 15 minutes or in the refrigerator for up to 12 hours.

Place the lettuce in a large bowl. Peel the cucumber and halve lengthwise. Scrape out the seeds with the tip of a spoon, then quarter each seeded half lengthwise to make 8 long strips. Cut the strips crosswise into pieces about ½ inch (12 mm) wide. Add to the bowl with the lettuce. Add the onion and herbs and toss to mix.

Remove the steak from the dressing and set aside on a plate. Pour the dressing over the salad and toss to coat thoroughly.

Pile the salad attractively on a platter or divide among individual plates. Arrange the steak strips on top, sprinkle with the peanuts, and serve.

Rice Noodles with Cucumber & Crab

The success of this Southeast Asian salad depends on the availability of fresh lump crabmeat. If your fishmonger doesn't have it, subsitute fresh, cooked shrimp for the crab. A mandoline is handy for shaving the cucumber into paper-thin slices, but a sharp knife will do the job too.

SERVES 4

1 Tbsp kosher salt

½ lb (250 g) dried flat rice noodles, about ¼ inch (6 mm) wide

¼ cup (2 fl oz/60 ml) coconut milk

2–3 Tbsp Asian fish sauce

Grated zest of 1 lime

2 Tbsp fresh lime juice

2–4 Thai chiles, sliced (optional)

1 cup (1 oz/30 g) mung bean sprouts

½ English cucumber, cut into paper-thin slices

½ lb (250 g) fresh lump crabmeat, picked over for shell and cartilage and flaked

½ cup (½ oz/15 g) fresh cilantro leaves

In a large pot, bring 4 quarts (4 l) water to a rapid boil. Add the salt and the noodles, stir well, and cook, stirring occasionally, until just tender, 3–5 minutes. Drain in a colander, place under cold running water to cool, and drain again thoroughly. In a bowl, stir together the coconut milk, fish sauce to taste, lime zest, lime juice, and chiles to taste (if using). Add the bean sprouts, cucumber, and crabmeat and toss gently to combine.

Transfer the noodles to a large, shallow serving bowl. Arrange the crab mixture over the noodles. Scatter the cilantro on top. Serve at room temperature or cover and refrigerate for up to 3 hours and serve chilled.

Salade Niçoise with Grilled Salmon

This updated recipe for the classic French salad calls for grilled salmon fillet, but you can use grilled ahi tuna instead. Make sure that each ingredient is of the highest quality, and you will sit down to a simple, stellar brunch, lunch, or light summer supper for two.

SERVES 2

6 small new potatoes

1 handful haricots verts, trimmed

Basic Vinaigrette (page 103) with red wine vinegar

1 handful mixed salad greens, about 2½–3 oz (75–90 g)

½ lb (250 g) mixed tomatoes, cut into slices, wedges, or halves

Salt and freshly ground pepper

2 large hard-boiled eggs (page 248), peeled and halved

15 Niçoise olives, rinsed and pitted

1 small wedge red onion, thinly sliced

2 anchovy fillets, rinsed in cold water and patted dry

Olive oil for brushing

6 oz (185 g) center-cut salmon fillet

Bring a large pot of salted water to boil. Add the potatoes and cook just until tender, 12–15 minutes. Using a slotted spoon, transfer the potatoes to a colander and let drain, then set aside to cool. Add the haricots verts to the boiling water and cook until tender but firm, 3–5 minutes, then drain in the colander and let cool.

Prepare a charcoal or gas grill for direct grilling over medium-high heat. Brush and oil the grill grate. (Alternatively, preheat a stove-top grill pan over medium-high heat.) Meanwhile, make the vinaigrette.

Place the greens in a salad bowl and drizzle with the vinaigrette, reserving some vinaigrette for drizzling on the salmon. Divide the dressed greens evenly between two plates. Lightly salt the tomatoes. Place small piles of the potatoes, haricots verts, tomatoes, egg quarters, olives, onion slices, and anchovies on the plates, dividing them evenly and leaving room for the salmon.

Brush the salmon all over with olive oil. Sprinkle with salt and pepper. Grill the fish over the hottest part of the fire, turning once, until it is opaque throughout and flakes when prodded with a fork, 3–5 minutes per side.

Divide the salmon evenly between the plates. Drizzle with the remaining vinaigrette and serve.

MODERN
HEIRLOOM

FRESH IN THE KITCHEN

INDULGE IN THE BEST INGREDIENTS

Vibrant greens, sweet summer corn, colorful autumn squashes, and more fill vendors' tables at your local farmers' market. Be adventuresome and pick out a few vegetables and fruits you've never tried before. Carrying home bags laden with top-notch produce delivers valuable rewards. Not only will your meals be healthful and delicious, but when you share time buying and preparing great ingredients, you're also setting the stage for a lifetime of inspired cooking together.

Roasted Beet Salad with Hazelnuts, Pancetta & Roquefort

The sweetness of hazelnuts and the earthy tang of Roquefort cheese are a sublime pairing. But don't let this classic combination prevent you from playing with other possibilities to partner with the beets. Try pine nuts and crumbled ricotta salata or pistachios with shaved pecorino.

SERVES 4–6

3 beets, a mixture of red and golden, about 1 lb (500 g) total weight

¼ cup (1 oz/30 g) hazelnuts

2 oz (60 g) pancetta, cubed

Salt and freshly ground pepper

Large leaves of butter or romaine lettuce for serving

½ lemon

2 oz (60 g) Roquefort cheese, crumbled

1 Tbsp chopped fresh flat-leaf parsley

Preheat the oven to 450°F (230°C). Trim the beet tops, leaving about 1 inch (2.5 cm) of the stems to prevent the beets from bleeding. Place the beets in a baking dish and tent loosely with aluminum foil. Roast until just fork-tender, 30–60 minutes, depending on the size and age of the beets.

Meanwhile, toast the hazelnuts in a small, dry frying pan over medium-low heat and cook, stirring constantly, until the nuts are fragrant and just beginning to brown where the skins have flaked off, about 10 minutes. Immediately pour the nuts onto a clean dish towel. Gather up the corners of the towel and rub the nuts together until most of the skins come off (it's okay if some skin bits stick). Chop the nuts coarsely and set aside.

In a large, dry frying pan over medium heat, sauté the pancetta until crispy, about 15 minutes. Using a slotted spoon, transfer to paper towels to drain. Reserve the fat in the pan.

When the beets are fork-tender, remove from the oven and let cool. When cool enough to handle, rub off the skins with a paper towel. Cut the beets into slices or bite-size cubes, add them to the reserved fat in the pan, and toss to coat. Season with salt and pepper.

To serve, arrange the lettuce leaves on a platter or on individual plates. Mound the beets on the lettuce leaves and squeeze lemon juice over the beets. Scatter the cheese, hazelnuts, and parsley over the top and serve.

North African Bulgur & Grilled Vegetable Salad

Bulgur is a versatile, fiber-rich, and easy-to-prepare whole grain that makes a great base for salads, pilafs, or sides. Here, it's mixed with a garden's worth of good-for-you vegetables in a salad that can be a main dish when accompanied with pita or crusty bread.

SERVES 4

8–10 spears asparagus, tough ends removed

2 zucchini, trimmed and cut on the diagonal into slices about ¼ inch (6 mm) thick

1 tsp extra-virgin olive oil

1½ cups (9 oz/280 g) bulgur wheat

FOR THE VINAIGRETTE

3 Tbsp extra-virgin olive oil

2 tsp grated lemon zest

2 Tbsp fresh lemon juice

2 tsp ground cumin

½ tsp ground turmeric

½ tsp cardamom seeds, crushed

Salt and freshly ground pepper

1 cup (7 oz/220 g) drained cooked or canned chickpeas

2 green onions, including tender green tops, thinly sliced

30 fresh mint leaves, minced

2 Tbsp minced fresh flat-leaf parsley

Prepare a charcoal or gas grill for direct grilling over medium heat. Brush and oil the grill grate. (Alternatively, preheat a grill pan over medium heat.)

Bring a teakettle full of water to a boil. Put the asparagus and zucchini in a heatproof bowl, add boiling water to cover, and let stand for 2 minutes to soften slightly. Drain, let cool, and toss with the olive oil. Put the bulgur in a heatproof bowl and add boiling water to cover by 2 inches (5 cm). Let stand for 10 minutes.

Meanwhile, grill the asparagus and zucchini, placing them perpendicular to the grill grate and turning often, until lightly browned and tender-crisp on all sides, 4–5 minutes. Transfer to a cutting board and let cool slightly. Cut the asparagus spears on the diagonal into thirds.

To make the vinaigrette, in a bowl, whisk together the olive oil, lemon zest and juice, cumin, turmeric, cardamom, 1 teaspoon salt, and several grinds of pepper. Stir the chickpeas into the vinaigrette, then transfer to a microwave-safe bowl and microwave on high for 1 minute to allow the flavors to blend. (Alternatively, in a saucepan over medium heat, warm the chickpeas and the vinaigrette, stirring occasionally, for a couple of minutes.)

Drain the bulgur. Combine the grilled vegetables, bulgur, green onions, mint, and parsley with the chickpeas and vinaigrette in a large serving bowl and toss to distribute and coat evenly. Serve warm or at room temperature.

Grain Salads

Cooked whole grains and grain-shaped pasta make a universally appealing base for a quartet of grab-and-go salads for two. Layer the grains in pint-size jars with the best fresh vegetables, fruits, and herbs you can find, then cover and go—whether to work or a picnic. Add the vinaigrette just before serving.

Beet, Bell Pepper & Orzo

1½ cups (10 oz/315 g) cooked and drained orzo or other rice-shaped pasta • 1½ Tbsp Dijon Vinaigrette (page 248) ⅔ cup (3½ oz/105 g) diced orange or red bell pepper ¾ cup (2½ oz/75 g) thinly sliced red cabbage • 1 cup (about 5 oz/155 g) cooked and halved or quartered assorted baby beets • Watercress or baby arugula sprigs for garnish

In a bowl, toss the warm orzo with the vinaigrette. Let cool. Divide the bell pepper equally between 2 jars. Top with the orzo. Layer the red cabbage and beets on top and garnish with watercress sprigs.

Mango, Avocado & Wheat Berry

1½ cups (8 oz/125 g) cooked and drained wheat berries 1½ Tbsp Dijon Vinaigrette (page 248) • ½ cup (2½ oz/75 g) shredded carrot • 3 Tbsp torn Thai or other fresh basil leaves, plus 2 small sprigs for garnish • 1 mango, diced 1 avocado, diced

In a bowl, toss the warm wheat berries with the vinaigrette. Let cool. Divide the carrot equally between 2 jars. Top with the wheat berries and torn basil. Layer the mango and avocado on top and garnish with basil sprigs.

Pea, Feta & Barley

1½ cups (8 oz/125 g) cooked and drained barley
1½ Tbsp Dijon Vinaigrette (page 248) • 4 radishes, thinly
sliced • 1 cup (5 oz/155 g) cooked fresh peas, cooled,
or frozen peas, thawed • ¼ cup (1 oz/30 g) crumbled
feta or soft goat cheese • Pea shoots for garnish

In a bowl, toss the warm barley with the vinaigrette.
Let cool. Divide the mixture equally between 2 jars.
Layer the radishes and peas over the barley and top
with the cheese. Garnish with pea shoots.

Orange, Cucumber & Couscous

1½ cups (8 oz/125 g) cooked and drained Israeli couscous
1½ Tbsp Dijon Vinaigrette (page 248) • ⅛ tsp ground cumin
1 green onion, chopped • 3 Tbsp coarsely chopped mint leaves,
plus 2 small sprigs for garnish • 1 seedless orange, peeled
and cut crosswise into ¼-inch (6-mm) thick slices • 2 Persian
cucumbers, cut into bite-size chunks • Toasted walnuts

In a bowl, toss the warm couscous with the vinaigrette and
cumin. Let cool. Divide the mixture equally between 2 jars.
Sprinkle green onion and mint over the couscous. Layer the
orange slices and cucumber and top with a sprinkling of
toasted walnuts. Garnish each salad with a mint sprig.

Chinese Chicken Salad with Sesame-Lime Vinaigrette

Thin slices of grilled chicken, crisp slivers of fried wontons, and fresh napa cabbage combine in this chicken salad classic. It's delicious as is, or include other common ingredients—cucumber, mung bean sprouts, mandarin oranges, or shaved almonds—according to preference.

SERVES 4–6

FOR THE VINAIGRETTE

¾ cup (6 fl oz/180 ml) fresh lime juice

¼ cup (2 fl oz/60 ml) seasoned rice vinegar

2 Tbsp Dijon mustard

2 Tbsp sugar

1½ tsp salt

⅔ cup (5 fl oz/160 ml) Asian sesame oil

½ cup (4 fl oz/125 ml) plus 1½ Tbsp canola oil

5 wonton skins, cut into strips ½ inch (12 mm) wide

Salt and freshly ground pepper

2 boneless, skinless chicken breast halves

1 head napa cabbage, halved lengthwise, cored, and sliced crosswise

4 green onions, including tender green tops, thinly sliced

¼ cup (1 oz/30 g) black sesame seeds

¼ cup (⅓ oz/10 g) finely chopped fresh cilantro

To make the vinaigrette, combine all the ingredients in a small jar and shake vigorously. Taste and adjust the seasoning and shake again. Set aside.

In a small nonstick frying pan over medium-high heat, warm the ½ cup (4 fl oz/125 ml) canola oil until just shimmering. Test the heat with a wonton strip, which should brown in about 30 seconds. Add the wontons and fry, using tongs to turn often, until lightly golden on both sides, 2–3 minutes total. Transfer to paper towels to drain and sprinkle with salt. Set aside.

Prepare a charcoal or gas grill for direct grilling over high heat and oil the grill grate, or preheat a stove-top grill pan over high heat. Using a chef's knife, cut each chicken breast half horizontally into 3 thin slices. Drizzle each slice on both sides with the 1½ tablespoons canola oil and season well with salt and pepper.

Arrange the chicken slices on the grill grate or in the grill pan and grill, turning once, until cooked through, about 3½ minutes per side. Transfer to a plate and let cool, then cut across the grain into slices.

To assemble the salad, in a large serving bowl, combine the cabbage, chicken, green onions, sesame seeds, 2 teaspoons salt, and 1 teaspoon pepper. Set aside 1 tablespoon of the cilantro and add the rest to the bowl. Drizzle some of the vinaigrette over the salad and toss to coat thoroughly. Taste and adjust the seasoning, adding more vinaigrette, if needed. Pile the crispy wontons on top of the salad, sprinkle with the reserved cilantro, and serve.

Little Gem Caesar Salad with White Anchovies

You'll need to track down the mild brined white anchovies, or boquerones, a pantry staple in Spain, for this salad, but you'll be rewarded with their exceptional flavor. Take the time to chill the salad plates to keep the salad cool, refreshing, and crisp as you eat it.

SERVES 4

FOR THE GARLIC CROUTONS

2 Tbsp extra-virgin olive oil

1 large clove garlic, crushed and minced

¼ loaf day-old rustic sourdough wheat bread or white French bread

Salt

FOR THE DRESSING

1 large egg

2 Tbsp fresh lemon juice

½ tsp Worcestershire sauce

1 tsp red wine vinegar

1½ Tbsp chopped white anchovy fillets

1 small clove garlic, minced

½ cup (4 fl oz/125 ml) extra-virgin olive oil

½ cup (2 oz/60 g) freshly grated Parmesan cheese

Salt and freshly ground pepper

2 heads Little Gem lettuce, leaves separated and torn into bite-size pieces

Parmesan cheese for shaving

Preheat the oven to 350°F (180°C).

To make the garlic croutons, in a medium bowl, whisk together the oil and garlic until combined. Tear the bread into about 20 bite-size pieces and add to the oil-garlic mixture with a pinch of salt. Toss the bread until coated, then spread the pieces on a baking sheet in a single layer. Toast, stirring occasionally, until the pieces are golden brown, 9–12 minutes. Let cool completely.

To make the dressing, crack the egg into a small bowl. Add the lemon juice, Worcestershire sauce, vinegar, anchovies, and garlic and whisk to combine well. Gradually whisk in the olive oil. Stir in the grated cheese. Season to taste with salt and pepper.

In a large bowl, combine the lettuce, croutons, and dressing and toss well. Divide the salad among 4 chilled plates. Using a vegetable peeler, shave thin curls of Parmesan over each salad and serve.

fresh eggs

The use of raw eggs is a good way to emulsify and add flavor to dressings. If you are pregnant or nursing, avoid the risk of salmonella and substitute Basic Vinaigrette (page 103) instead.

emperor's rice bowl

Black rice, sometimes referred to as Emperor's Rice or Forbidden Rice, is loaded with the same powerful antioxidant prevalent in blueberries, dark purple eggplant, and açai berries.

Asparagus, Pea, Radish & Black Rice Salad

Asparagus, snow peas, sugar snaps, and radishes—early gifts from the garden—make this vibrant salad a celebration of spring. If you cannot find black rice, brown or white rice can be substituted. If it's just for the two of you, store the salad before you add the dressing and the nuts, then add them just before serving.

SERVES 4–6

6 snow peas, trimmed

6 sugar snap peas, strings removed

4 fat asparagus, thinly sliced diagonally

2 cups (10 oz/315 g) cooked black rice, preferably Black Japonica or Forbidden variety

3 large red radishes, thinly sliced

3 Tbsp shelled pistachios, coarsely chopped

2 Tbsp fresh tarragon, chopped

1½ Tbsp white wine vinegar

1 tsp salt

Freshly ground pepper

1½ Tbsp avocado oil or canola oil

Bring a large pot of water to a boil. Prepare a large bowl of ice water.

Blanch the snow peas, sugar snap peas, and asparagus in the boiling water for 30 seconds. Immediately drain the vegetables, then cool them in the ice water. Spread them on paper towels and pat dry.

Halve the snow peas lengthwise and place in a large bowl. Add the snap peas, asparagus, rice, radishes, pistachios, and tarragon to the bowl.

In a small bowl, whisk the vinegar, salt, and a few grinds of pepper until the salt dissolves. Whisk in the oil. Pour the dressing over the rice salad and toss gently with a fork. Serve right away, or refrigerate in an airtight container for up to 8 hours.

Fennel Salad with Blood Oranges & Arugula

To ensure the fennel remains crisp, keep the bulbs cold until you're ready to slice them, which should be just before serving. Cut fennel will discolor, so dress it right away or submerge it in cold water. Round out the menu with a plate of cheeses and cold meats and some crusty bread.

SERVES 6–8

2 fennel bulbs

2 Tbsp red wine vinegar

Salt and freshly ground pepper

6 Tbsp (3 fl oz/90 ml) extra-virgin olive oil

4 cups (4 oz/125 g) loosely packed arugula leaves

4 blood or navel oranges, peeled with a knife and sliced crosswise into thin slices

Trim the stem ends and feathery fronds from the fennel bulbs, reserving a few of the fronds for garnish. Halve the fennel bulbs lengthwise and, using a mandoline or a very sharp knife, cut the halves crosswise into paper-thin slices.

In a large bowl, whisk together the vinegar, ¼ teaspoon salt, and ¼ teaspoon pepper. Add the olive oil in a thin stream, whisking constantly until the dressing is smooth. Add the arugula and sliced fennel and toss to coat evenly with the vinaigrette. Mound the mixture on a platter, distribute the orange slices over and around the salad, sprinkle the fronds over the top, and serve.

supreme citrus

To cut the oranges into wheels, cut
off the peel at both ends. Stand the
orange upright. Cut off the peel in
strips, following the contour of the
fruit, then cut the fruit into slices.

CHAPTER FOUR

PASTA, PIZZA & RISOTTO

We go together like tomato sauce and pasta

Orecchiette with Sausage & Broccoli Rabe

Orecchiette, literally "little ears," trap the morsels of sausage and bits of greens in this typical Puglian sauce, but other short pastas with grooves or hollows work well, too. If you prefer a little heat, use spicy Italian sausage instead of the sweet sausage.

SERVES 4–6

1 Tbsp garlic-infused olive oil

¼ cup (⅓ oz/10 g) panko bread crumbs

Salt and freshly ground black pepper

2 lb (1 kg) broccoli rabe

6 Tbsp (3 fl oz/90 ml) extra-virgin olive oil

¾ lb (375 g) sweet Italian sausages, casings removed

4 cloves garlic, minced

Pinch of red pepper flakes

1 lb (500 g) orecchiette, cavatelli, or gnocchetti

Freshly grated Parmesan cheese for serving

In a wide frying pan over medium-low heat, warm the garlic oil. Add the bread crumbs and cook, stirring, until golden, 2–3 minutes. Transfer the crumbs to a small bowl, season to taste with salt and pepper, and set aside.

Using a small, sharp knife or vegetable peeler, peel away the thick skin from the tough lower stalks of the broccoli rabe (most of the bottom stalk portion). Cut crosswise into about 1-inch (2.5-cm) lengths. Place in a bowl, add cold water to cover, and let stand for 1 hour.

In a large pot, bring 5 qt (5 l) salted water to a boil. Add the broccoli rabe, cover partially, and cook for 1 minute after the water returns to a boil. Using a wire skimmer, transfer the broccoli rabe to a bowl and set aside. Reserve ½ cup (4 fl oz/125 ml) of the cooking water and set aside. Reserve the remaining water in the pot.

In a large frying pan over medium-low heat, warm 2 tablespoons of the olive oil. Add the sausage and cook, stirring to break up any clumps, until evenly browned, about 10 minutes. Add the garlic and red pepper flakes and cook, stirring occasionally, until the garlic is softened, about 3 minutes. Add the broccoli rabe and the reserved ½ cup (4 fl oz/125 ml) cooking water and toss to mix. Cover and cook, stirring occasionally, until the greens are tender, 8–10 minutes.

Meanwhile, return the water in the pot to a boil. Add the pasta and cook according to the package directions.

Drain the pasta and add to the sauce in the pan. Add the remaining 4 tablespoons (2 fl oz/60 ml) olive oil and toss to coat. Season with salt and transfer to a serving bowl. Sprinkle with the bread crumbs and Parmesan, and serve.

Any leftovers from this wholesome pot
can taste even better the next day,
so make this flavorful pasta as a
weeknight dinner for two and have
enough left over for lunch.

Baked Gnocchi with Taleggio & Pancetta

Here's a weeknight supper that relies on store-bought fresh pasta, comes together in minutes, and can even be readied for baking and refrigerated the night before serving. You can substitute 1 pound (500 g) penne for the gnocchi and fontina for the Taleggio.

SERVES 4

2 packages (13 oz/410 g each) fresh gnocchi

½ lb (250 g) Taleggio cheese

Butter for greasing

¼ lb (125 g) sliced pancetta, cut into ½-inch (12-mm) pieces

2 Tbsp chopped fresh sage

1½ cups (12 fl oz/375 ml) half-and-half

¼ cup (1 oz/30 g) dried bread crumbs

Freshly ground pepper

Cook the gnocchi according to the package directions. Drain and set aside.

Meanwhile, trim the rind off the cheese and cut the cheese into ¼-inch (6-mm) cubes. Set aside.

Preheat the oven to 375°F (190°C). Butter four 7-inch (18-cm) shallow oval baking dishes.

In a large, cold frying pan, place the pancetta in a single layer. Cook over medium heat until the pancetta starts to brown, about 2 minutes. Using a spatula, turn over and continue to cook until browned, about 2 minutes longer. Remove the pan from the heat and stir in the gnocchi, sage, half-and-half, and cheese.

Transfer the gnocchi mixture to the prepared baking dishes, dividing it evenly. Sprinkle the tops with bread crumbs and season with a few grinds of pepper. At this point, the gnocchi can be cooled to room temperature, covered with plastic wrap, and refrigerated for up to 24 hours. Remove from the refrigerator 30 minutes before baking.

Bake the gnocchi until golden, about 15 minutes. Serve hot, directly from the oven.

The Ultimate
Mac & Cheese

*This mac and cheese is a modern take on a childhood favorite.
It's a big casserole, so either invite your neighbors over or
plan to reheat the leftovers: Drizzle with a splash of milk, cover
with aluminum foil, and slip into a 350°F (180°C) oven.*

SERVES 6

7 Tbsp (3½ oz/105 g) unsalted butter,
plus more for greasing

1 clove garlic, minced

1½ cups (3 oz/90 g) coarse fresh bread
crumbs

Kosher salt and freshly ground pepper

1 lb (500 g) elbow macaroni

¼ cup (1½ oz/45 g) all-purpose flour

3 cups (24 fl oz/750 ml) whole milk,
warmed

2 cups (8 oz/250 g) shredded sharp
Cheddar cheese

2 cups (8 oz/250 g) shredded fontina
cheese

½ tsp dry mustard

make it your own

Any tubular pasta works well in this
recipe. Some favorites are penne,
ziti, or mostaccioli. You can also try
adding chopped crisp bacon, cubes
of smoked ham or cooked chicken,
cooked peas, chopped blanched
broccoli, sautéed wild mushrooms,
or crumbled blue cheese when
you stir in the cheese.

In a large frying pan over medium-low heat, melt
3 tablespoons of the butter. Add the garlic and cook,
stirring frequently, until tender but not browned,
about 3 minutes. Add the bread crumbs and stir until
coated with butter. Set aside.

Bring a large pot of salted water to a boil. Add the pasta,
stir, and cook according to the package directions, stirring
occasionally, until not quite al dente. (The macaroni will
cook again in the oven, so do not overcook it now.) Drain
well and set aside.

Preheat the oven to 350°F (180°C). Butter a shallow
3-qt (3-l) baking dish.

In the pot used for the pasta over medium heat, melt the
remaining 4 tablespoons (2 oz/60 g) butter. Whisk in
the flour. Reduce the heat to medium-low and let bubble
for 1 minute without browning. Gradually whisk in the
milk, raise the heat to medium, and bring to a boil,
whisking frequently. Remove from the heat and stir in
the cheeses and the mustard. Season with salt and
pepper. Stir in the pasta. Spread in the prepared baking
dish and sprinkle evenly with the buttered crumbs.

Bake until the crumbs are browned and the sauce is
bubbling, about 20 minutes. Let cool for 5 minutes,
then serve hot.

chile

bacon

basil

garlic

cheese

tomato

Pizza Four Ways

Once you've mastered the dough (recipe on page 250), making freshly baked pizza at home is as easy as pie. Use a pizza peel or rimless baking sheet to slide the topped dough onto a hot pizza stone for the best crust.

pizza method

Make homemade pizza dough (page 250) or purchase enough dough for two pizzas. Remove the dough from the refrigerator 1 to 2 hours before rolling it out.

Position a rack in the lower third of the oven. Place a pizza stone on the rack and preheat the oven to 450°F (230°C), allowing at least 30 minutes at cooking temperature for the oven to heat fully. Meanwhile, prepare the toppings.

Divide the dough in half and shape each half into a taut ball. Place 1 ball on a lightly floured work surface. Cover the remaining ball with a kitchen towel and set aside. Roll, pat, and stretch the dough into a round about 12 inches (30 cm) in diameter.

Generously dust a pizza peel with cornmeal. Transfer the dough round to the peel and reshape as needed. Choose a topping at right; each topping recipe makes enough for one pizza.

Slide the pizza off the peel onto the hot stone. Bake until the crust is golden, about 12 minutes. While the first pizza is baking, repeat to shape and top the remaining round. Using the pizza peel, a wide spatula, or a rimless baking sheet, remove the baked pizza from the oven and transfer to a cutting board. Repeat to top and bake the remaining dough round. Cut the pizzas and serve.

MAKES 2 PIZZAS

brussels sprouts
+
bacon

6 strips lightly fried bacon, chopped

¾ cup (2 oz/60 g) halved and thinly sliced Brussels sprouts

1 Tbsp olive oil

Salt and freshly ground pepper

1 cup (8 oz/250 g) tomato sauce

8 oz (250 g) fresh mozzarella cheese, diced

Toss the Brussels sprouts and bacon with the oil to coat, then season with salt and pepper. Top the pizza dough with the tomato sauce and mozzarella, then with the Brussels sprouts mixture.

artichoke
+
spinach
+
tapenade

¾ cup (6 fl oz/180 ml) olive tapenade

1 cup (4 oz/125 g) shredded low-moisture mozzarella cheese

½ cup (4 oz/125 g) sautéed spinach

½ cup (4 oz/125 g) sliced artichoke hearts, drained

10-15 cherry tomatoes, halved

Spread the tapenade over the dough round and top with the cheese. Distribute the spinach, artichoke hearts, and tomatoes evenly on top.

roasted squash
+
sage

1 large butternut squash, peeled, seeded, and cubed

2 Tbsp olive oil

1½ cups (6 oz/185 g) shredded smoked mozzarella cheese

8 fresh sage leaves

Preheat oven to 450°F (230°C). Toss the squash with the oil to coat, spread on a baking sheet, and roast, stirring once, until caramelized, about 30 minutes. Sprinkle the cheese and squash evenly over the pizza dough and scatter the sage leaves on top.

fennel sausage
+
ricotta
+
fresh tomato

1 cup (4 oz/125 g) shredded low-moisture mozzarella cheese

3 ripe plum tomatoes, thinly sliced

½ lb (250 g) fennel sausage, removed from casings

½ cup (4 oz/125 g) whole-milk ricotta cheese

Fresh basil leaves for garnish

Top the pizza dough with the mozzarella, then the tomatoes. Crumble the sausage evenly over the top, then dollop with the ricotta. Sprinkle with basil after baking.

Basic Egg Pasta Dough

A food processor makes short work of mixing the dough for fresh pasta. You'll need a classic hand-cranked pasta machine for the next step in this method—one in which the fresh dough is folded and fed through the rollers, rendering it smooth and easily pliable.

MAKES 1 LB (500 G)

2 cups (10 oz/315 g) unbleached all-purpose flour, plus more as needed

1 Tbsp semolina flour, plus more for dusting

½ tsp salt

Pinch of freshly grated nutmeg

3 extra-large eggs, lightly beaten

1–2 Tbsp olive oil

dust well

It can be frustrating trying to disengage pieces of pasta that stick together after they have been cut. Avoid any potential problems by sprinkling freshly cut dough with a liberal dose of semolina flour, then carefully set the pasta aside until you are ready to cook.

In a food processor, combine the flours, salt, and nutmeg and pulse briefly to mix. Add the eggs and process briefly. Drizzle in 1 tablespoon of the olive oil and process until the mixture forms curd-like crumbs. When you pinch the dough, it should form a soft ball. If it is too wet or sticky, add more flour, 1 tablespoon at a time, and process briefly. If it is too dry, drizzle in the remaining 1 tablespoon olive oil.

Turn the dough out onto a floured work surface and knead until smooth and firm but pliable, about 10 minutes. Wrap the dough tightly in plastic wrap and let stand at room temperature for 30 minutes.

Cut the dough into 4 equal pieces. Cover 3 pieces with plastic wrap. Briefly knead the fourth piece on a lightly floured surface. Set the rollers of a pasta machine to the widest setting, then crank the dough through the rollers. Fold the dough into thirds as you would a letter for an envelope and pass it through the rollers again, open end first. Repeat folding and rolling two or three times until the dough is smooth. Reset the rollers one width narrower and crank the dough through the setting twice, then adjust the rollers to the next narrowest setting. Continue to pass the dough through the rollers twice on each setting until you have a long, thin sheet, rolling to ⅛-inch (3-mm) thickness for cut noodles, or 1/16-inch (2-mm) thickness for ravioli.

To cut noodles, using the cutting attachment of the pasta machine or a pastry cutter, cut the pasta sheet into the desired width. Toss with semolina flour and set aside.

To make ravioli, lay the dough sheet on a floured work surface. Spoon tablespoons of filling at 3½-inch (9-cm) intervals along the center of the dough sheet, leaving half of the sheet uncovered. Dip your finger in water and lightly moisten the edges of the dough and the area between the mounds. Fold the uncovered half on top and gently press between the mounds to seal. Using a pastry cutter, cut out large ravioli, each about 3½ inches (9 cm) square.

Repeat with the remaining 3 dough pieces. Cook as directed.

Sauce Arsenal

With this quartet of classic sauces, you have all you need to create hundreds of Italian dishes—from pasta and pizza to main courses featuring meat, vegetables, or shellfish.

Bolognese

2 Tbsp olive oil • 1 carrot, peeled and finely diced • 1 rib celery, finely diced • ½ yellow onion, finely diced • Salt and freshly ground pepper • 3 cloves garlic, chopped • ½ lb (250 g) *each* ground beef and ground veal • 2 oz (60 g) pancetta, finely diced • ½ cup (4 fl oz/125 ml) dry red wine • 3 Tbsp tomato paste • 2–3 cups (16–24 fl oz/500–750 ml) beef broth

In a heavy, nonreactive saucepan over medium-high heat, warm the olive oil. Add the carrot, celery, and onion and season with salt and pepper. Sauté until the vegetables are soft, about 7 minutes. Add the garlic and sauté just until soft, about 1 minute longer. Add the beef, veal, and pancetta, and season with salt and pepper. Cook, stirring often and using a spoon to break up any clumps, until the meat is browned, about 10 minutes. Add the wine and cook until the liquid is reduced by about half, about 4 minutes. Stir in the tomato paste and 2 cups (16 fl oz/500 ml) of the

beef broth and season with salt and pepper. Bring to a boil, then reduce the heat to low to maintain a gentle simmer. Cover partially and cook for 45 minutes, checking every 15 minutes or so that there is enough liquid for the sauce to braise. Add more broth, ¼ cup (2 fl oz/60 ml) at a time, if needed. Remove the pan from the heat. Taste and adjust the seasoning. Use immediately, or let cool and refrigerate in an airtight container for up to 1 week, or freeze for up to 2 months.

MAKES ABOUT 2½ CUPS (20 FL OZ/625 ML)

Herb Pesto

1 clove garlic • 2 Tbsp pine nuts • 2½ cups
(2½ oz/75 g) baby arugula or fresh basil
leaves • ¼ cup (1 oz/30 g) freshly grated
Parmesan cheese • ½ cup (4 fl oz/125 ml)
extra-virgin olive oil • Salt and freshly
ground pepper

In a food processor, combine the garlic,
pine nuts, arugula or basil, and cheese
and pulse to chop finely. With the machine
running, add the olive oil in a slow and
steady stream. Season with salt and a
few grinds of pepper. Use immediately,
or let cool, and refrigerate in an airtight
container for up to 1 week (some
discoloration may occur during storage).

MAKES ABOUT 1 CUP (8 FL OZ/250 ML)

Alfredo

2 cups (16 fl. oz./500 ml) heavy cream
½ cup (4 oz/125 g) unsalted butter • 1 cup
(4 oz/125 g) freshly grated Parmesan
cheese • Salt and freshly ground pepper
Pinch of freshly grated nutmeg

In a saucepan over medium-low heat,
warm the cream. In another saucepan
over medium heat, melt the butter.
Add the warmed cream and stir in the
cheese. Season with salt, pepper, and
nutmeg. Bring the sauce to a gentle
simmer and cook just until it thickens
slightly, about 2 minutes.

MAKES ABOUT 3 CUPS
(24 FL OZ/750 ML)

Heirloom Tomato

3 lb (1.5 kg) heirloom tomatoes
¼ small red or yellow onion, finely
sliced or chopped • ¾ cup (¾ oz/30 g)
firmly packed fresh basil leaves,
roughly torn • ½ tsp salt

Core the tomatoes, then cut them into
halves, remove the seeds with your
fingers, and chop coarsely. In a large
saucepan over medium-high heat,
combine the tomatoes, onion, basil,
and salt. Bring to a boil, then reduce
the heat to medium and simmer,
stirring often to prevent sticking,
until thickened, about 20 minutes.

MAKES ABOUT 2 CUPS
(16 FL OZ/500 ML)

PLAN AHEAD

PREP INGREDIENTS FOR EASY COOKING

Whether you are chopping vegetables, whisking eggs,
or greasing a baking dish, organizing what you
need before you begin to cook makes every meal,
from supper for two to a dinner party for eight,
come together more smoothly. The French call this process
mise en place—literally "set in place"—and savvy cooks
everywhere know that assembling ingredients
and equipment in advance of cooking guarantees a more
relaxed—and more fun—time together in the kitchen.

mix of greens

Any combination of bitter greens can star in this filling. Use a mix of escarole, chicory, and dandelion greens, or try radicchio for an unusual yet delicious riff.

Ravioli with Bitter Greens & Toasted Walnut Butter

If you've had a busy week and still crave these scrumptious ravioli, look for thin fresh pasta sheets at an Italian specialty store or high-end supermarket to save time and effort.

MAKES 24–28 LARGE RAVIOLI; SERVES 6–8

FOR THE FILLING

2 Tbsp unsalted butter

1 Tbsp olive oil

2 shallots, diced

1 lb (500 g) bitter greens (see note at left), cores and thick stems removed, then cut crosswise into shreds

Salt and freshly ground pepper

1 Tbsp fresh lemon juice

½ cup (4 oz/125 g) well-drained ricotta

¼ lb (125 g) fresh mozzarella cheese, cut into small cubes

FOR THE PASTA

Basic Egg Pasta Dough (page 131)

FOR THE WALNUT BUTTER

1½ cups (12 oz/375 g) salted butter

¾ cup (3 oz/90 g) coarsely chopped walnuts, lightly toasted

2 Tbsp fresh lemon juice

2 Tbsp minced fresh flat-leaf parsley

½ cup (2 oz/60 g) freshly grated pecorino romano cheese

To make the filling, in a large frying pan over medium heat, melt the butter with the olive oil. Add the shallots and cook, stirring often, until tender, about 5 minutes. Add as many handfuls of greens as you can and sprinkle with ¼ teaspoon salt. Cover and cook until the greens start to wilt, about 2 minutes. Uncover, stir, and add more greens. Repeat until all are added. Sprinkle with ¼ teaspoon salt and cook, uncovered, until the greens are soft, about 10 minutes longer. Stir in the lemon juice and season with pepper. Let cool briefly, then drain, pressing out the liquid. Transfer to a cutting board and chop finely. In a bowl, combine the greens and cheeses and mix well. Cover and refrigerate until ready to use.

To make the pasta, follow the directions for the basic egg pasta dough. Cut and fill the ravioli as directed.

Bring a large pot of salted water to a boil over high heat. Preheat the oven to 200°F (95°C).

Meanwhile, make the walnut butter: In a large saucepan over medium heat, melt the butter. When it begins to foam, swirl the pan and cook until it begins to brown. Reduce the heat to low and stir in the walnuts and lemon juice. Remove from the heat and cover. Spoon one-third of the walnut butter into a serving bowl and place in the oven.

Add half of the ravioli to the boiling water and cook until al dente, 3–5 minutes. Using a skimmer, transfer them to the serving bowl. Spoon a little of the remaining walnut butter from the pan over them and sprinkle with a little parsley and cheese. Return the bowl to the oven. Repeat to cook the remaining ravioli and transfer to the bowl. Spoon the remaining walnut butter on top, sprinkle with the remaining parsley and cheese, and serve.

Fettuccine with Peas, Lemon & Ricotta

In spring, when fresh peas are in season and good sheep's milk ricotta is at your favorite cheese shop, make this wholesome sauce, which can be assembled in the time it takes to bring pasta water to a boil.

SERVES 4

2 Tbsp unsalted butter

1 Tbsp olive oil

1 small white onion, finely diced

2 cups (10 oz/315 g) fresh or thawed frozen peas

Salt and freshly ground pepper

Grated zest of 2 lemons

1 lb (500 g) fettuccine

½ cup (4 oz/125 g) fresh sheep's milk or whole-milk ricotta, at room temperature

4 thin slices prosciutto, cut into julienne

½ cup (2 oz/60 g) freshly grated Parmesan cheese

Bring a large pot of salted water to a boil.

In a large frying pan over medium-low heat, melt the butter with the olive oil. Add the onion and sauté until soft and translucent, 7–8 minutes. Add the peas, stir to coat thoroughly, and cook until just tender and no longer raw-tasting, about 7 minutes. Stir in ½ teaspoon salt, a generous grinding of pepper, and the lemon zest and remove from the heat. Cover to keep warm and set aside.

Add the pasta to the boiling water, stir, and cook according to the package directions, stirring occasionally, until al dente. Drain, reserving about 1 cup (8 fl oz/250 ml) of the cooking water. Transfer the pasta to the pan with the sauce and toss gently to combine. Add as much of the cooking water as needed to loosen the sauce. Add the ricotta and prosciutto and toss gently to combine. Add the grated cheese and toss gently again. Taste and adjust the seasoning. Divide among individual shallow bowls and serve.

Weeknight Linguine Carbonara

You can make this pasta in a pinch when you need a wholesome supper in a hurry. It calls for only a few pantry staples and is at once quick and satisfying.

SERVES 2

½ lb (250 g) linguine, spaghettini, fedelini, or other long noodles

1 Tbsp olive oil

3 thick slices bacon, diced

2 large eggs

¼ tsp freshly grated nutmeg (optional)

Salt and freshly ground pepper

Freshly grated Parmesan cheese or pecorino romano for serving

Bring a large pot of salted water to a boil. Add the pasta, stir, and cook according to the package directions, stirring occasionally, until al dente.

While the pasta is cooking, in a medium sauté pan over medium heat, warm the olive oil and add the bacon. Sauté until browned and slightly crisp, 3–5 minutes. Pour off all but 1½ tablespoons of the fat. Set aside the pan with the bacon and reserved fat.

In a small bowl, beat the eggs with a fork to loosen them, add the nutmeg, if using, and season with salt.

Drain the pasta, reserving ¼ cup (2 fl oz/60 ml) of the pasta cooking water. Warm the pan with the bacon and add the pasta. Using tongs, thoroughly toss the pasta with the bacon and fat and season to taste with salt. Remove the pan from the heat, add the egg mixture, and quickly toss with the hot pasta to thicken the sauce without scrambling the eggs. If the sauce seems dry, add 1 or 2 tablespoons of the reserved pasta cooking water and toss again. Divide the pasta between warmed shallow bowls, grate the cheese and coarsely grind pepper over each bowl, and serve.

olive oil

corn

garlic

squash
blossoms

lemon

salt & pepper

basil

fennel
blossoms

Risotto Four Ways

In Italy, short-grain rice varieties, such as Arborio, Vialone Nano, and Carnaroli, are grown specifically for making risotto. You can prepare the risotto partially in advance and finish the cooking 15 minutes before serving.

classic risotto

3 Tbsp unsalted butter • 2 Tbsp minced shallots • 1 cup (7 oz/220 g) Arborio or Carnaroli rice • 2½ cups (20 fl oz/625 ml) meat or vegetable stock, heated ½ cup (4 fl oz/125 ml) dry Italian white wine • Generous pinch of powdered saffron (optional) • ¼ cup (1 oz/30 g) freshly grated Parmesan cheese Salt and freshly ground white pepper • Freshly grated nutmeg

In a deep saucepan over low heat, melt 2 tablespoons of the butter. Add the shallots and sauté until translucent, about 2 minutes. Stir in the rice, coating it thoroughly with the butter. Cook, stirring, until the edges of the grains are translucent, about 2 minutes.

Increase the heat to medium. Add 1 cup (8 fl oz/250 ml) of the stock and simmer, stirring occasionally, until the rice absorbs most of the stock with only a little visible liquid remaining, 5–6 minutes.

Add another 1 cup (8 fl oz/250 ml) stock, stir to mix, and again allow the rice to absorb most of the liquid, 5–6 minutes longer. At this point, the risotto can be removed from the heat and set aside for up to 2 hours.

Reduce the heat to medium-low, and stir in the wine and saffron (if using). Allow the rice to absorb most of the wine, stirring occasionally, 4–5 minutes longer. Add another ½ cup (4 fl oz/125 ml) stock and continue to simmer, stirring, for 4–5 minutes longer.

Stir in the cheese, the remaining 1 tablespoon butter, and season to taste with salt, white pepper, and nutmeg. The risotto should be al dente. If it is too moist, simmer for a few minutes longer; if it is too dry, stir in a little additional stock. Taste and adjust with more wine, cheese, and seasonings.

Remove from the heat when there is a little more liquid than desired, as the rice will continue to absorb it. Mound the risotto in shallow bowls and serve hot.

SERVES 4

porcini + garlic

Omit the saffron and nutmeg. Soak ½ cup (1 oz/30 g) dried porcini mushrooms in 1 cup (8 fl oz/250 ml) lukewarm water until soft, 20–30 minutes. Lift out the mushrooms, reserving the soaking liquid. Squeeze the mushrooms dry and chop them. Strain the soaking liquid through a cheesecloth-lined fine-mesh sieve, reserving ⅓ cup (2½ fl oz/75 ml) for the risotto. Add 2 minced garlic cloves to the rice with the first addition of stock. Add the chopped mushrooms and reserved soaking liquid when half the stock has been added.

asparagus + lemon + thyme

Omit the saffron and nutmeg. Steam ½ lb (250 g) trimmed asparagus spears until tender-crisp, 3–4 minutes, cut into 1-inch (2.5-cm) pieces, and set aside. Add 1 fresh thyme sprig to the shallots with the rice. Just after adding the cheese, stir in the reserved asparagus with 1 teaspoon lemon zest, 1 tablespoon lemon juice, and ¼ cup (2 fl oz/60 ml) heavy cream, then add the butter and season to taste.

fresh corn + basil oil

Omit the saffron and nutmeg. Add ¾ cup (4 oz/125 g) fresh corn kernels with the final addition of stock. Garnish each bowl with a sprinkling of chopped fresh chives and a drizzle of basil oil before serving.

squash blossoms + fennel

Omit the saffron and nutmeg. Cook the risotto as directed, adding 1 cup (1 oz/15 g) torn squash blossoms with the final addition of stock. Garnish each bowl with fresh fennel blossoms or fronds before serving.

Whole-Wheat Pappardelle with Mushrooms

For the best flavor, use fresh wild mushrooms such as chanterelles or black trumpets, cultivated mushrooms like shiitakes or oysters, or a combination. Avoid portobello or cremini mushrooms, which are too dry for this silky sauce.

MAKES 1 LB (500 G); SERVES 4

FOR THE PASTA

1½ cups (7½ oz/235 g) whole-wheat flour

½ cup (2½ oz/75 g) unbleached all-purpose flour, plus more for dusting

¼ tsp salt

3 large eggs, at room temperature

1 Tbsp olive or vegetable oil

1 cup (1 oz/30 g) dried porcini mushrooms, soaked in ½ cup (4 fl oz/125 ml) hot water for 30 minutes

¾ lb (375 g) mixed fresh wild or cultivated mushrooms (see note), tough stems removed

¼ cup (2 oz/60 g) unsalted butter

1 Tbsp olive oil

2 large shallots, minced

2 tsp chopped fresh thyme

Salt and freshly ground pepper

1 cup (8 fl oz/250 ml) heavy cream

To make the pasta, using the pasta ingredients here, follow the method for Basic Egg Pasta Dough (page 131), but increase the kneading time to 12–14 minutes. Roll out the dough and cut into ¾-inch (2-mm) wide strips. Drape the noodles on a pasta rack or the back of a chair and let dry for 30 minutes or up to 3 hours.

Remove the porcini from the water and reserve the soaking water. Rinse the porcini under cold running water to remove any grit and squeeze dry. Using scissors, cut into ½-inch (12-mm) pieces. Line a fine-mesh sieve with cheesecloth, place over a bowl, and strain the soaking water. Set the mushrooms and soaking water aside separately.

Thinly slice the caps and tender stems of the fresh mushrooms and set aside.

In a large frying pan over medium-low heat, melt the butter with the olive oil. Add the shallots and thyme and sauté until the shallots are softened, about 5 minutes. Add the porcini and sauté for about 5 minutes. Add the fresh mushrooms and sauté until tender, about 5 minutes longer. Add the soaking water, ½ teaspoon sea salt, and ¼ teaspoon pepper and simmer gently, stirring occasionally, for 5 minutes. Stir in the cream until small bubbles begin to form around the edges of the pan. Do not let the cream boil. Remove from the heat and cover to keep warm.

Bring a large pot of water to a boil. Add 2 tablespoons kosher salt and the pasta and cover the pot. When the water returns to a boil, uncover, cook for about 5 seconds, then drain. Add the pasta to the sauce in the pan and toss to coat well. Transfer to a large warmed bowl and serve.

White Lasagne with Mushrooms & Prosciutto

Earthy mushrooms and salty ham stud this baked pasta dish with bursts of flavor. This is a great dish for a dinner party because it can be made in advance: Assemble the lasagne, cover it tightly, and store it in the refrigerator for up to 1 day, then bake as directed.

SERVES 6–8

½ cup (4 oz/125 g) unsalted butter, plus more for greasing

½ cup (2½ oz/75 g) unbleached all-purpose flour

½ tsp freshly grated nutmeg

4 cups (32 fl oz/1 l) whole milk

1 cup (8 fl oz/250 ml) chicken stock or low-sodium broth

½ cup (4 fl oz/125 ml) Marsala

2 large eggs, lightly beaten

1¾ cups (7 oz/220 g) shredded fontina cheese

Salt and ground white pepper

4 Tbsp (2 fl oz/60 ml) olive oil

1 small leek, including tender green tops, thinly sliced

¾ lb (375 g) white button mushrooms, sliced

½ lb (250 g) thinly sliced prosciutto, chopped

2 Tbsp chopped fresh basil

12 no-boil lasagne noodles, or Basic Egg Pasta Dough (page 131), cut to fit the baking dish

½ cup (2 oz/60 g) freshly grated Parmesan cheese

Preheat the oven to 350°F (180°C). Butter an 8-by-11-inch (20-by-28-cm) baking dish.

In a large saucepan over medium-low heat, melt the butter. Stir in the flour and cook, whisking constantly, for about 3 minutes. Whisk in the nutmeg. Raise the heat to medium-high and gradually whisk in the milk and stock. Bring the mixture to a boil and continue whisking until thickened and smooth, 10–15 minutes. Remove from the heat and let cool, stirring occasionally, until warm. Stir in the Marsala, eggs, and 1 cup (4 oz/125 g) of the fontina until the cheese melts and the sauce is smooth. Season with salt and white pepper. Set aside.

In a large frying pan over medium-high heat, warm 2 tablespoons of the olive oil. Add the leek and sauté just until wilted, about 3 minutes. Transfer to a bowl. Add the remaining 2 tablespoons olive oil to the pan. When the oil is hot, add the mushrooms and sauté, stirring, until golden, about 5 minutes. Add the prosciutto and basil and cook, stirring, for 1 minute longer.

Spread about 1½ cups (12 fl oz/375 ml) of the cheese sauce evenly over the bottom of the prepared baking dish. Spoon about one-third of the mushroom mixture evenly over the sauce, then arrange 4 of the lasagne noodles over the top. Repeat these layers twice. Spread the remaining sauce over the top layer, then sprinkle the remaining ¾ cup (3 oz/95 g) fontina and the Parmesan evenly over the top. Bake until the top is golden and the juices are bubbling, about 45 minutes. Let the lasagne cool for 15–30 minutes, cut into squares, and serve.

Spaghettini with Cauliflower Pesto

Cauliflower is too often boiled, which hides its great taste and texture. Here it's charred to bring out its naturally nutty flavor, which works perfectly with pasta. If it's just dinner for two, refrigerate half of the pesto for an easy dinner on another night.

SERVES 4–6

1 small head cauliflower, cored and cut into 1-inch (2.5-cm) florets

Salt and freshly ground pepper

1 cup (8 fl oz/250 ml) extra-virgin olive oil

1 cup (1 oz/30 g) fresh flat-leaf parsley leaves

½ cup (2 oz/60 g) toasted almonds

2 Tbsp capers

2 cloves garlic, minced

1 lb (500 g) spaghettini

½ cup (2 oz/60 g) freshly grated Parmesan cheese

Preheat a stove-top grill pan over high heat.

Season the cauliflower florets with salt and pepper. Place on the grill pan and cook, turning occasionally, until well charred on all sides, 6–8 minutes. Transfer to a food processor and add the olive oil, parsley, almonds, capers, and garlic. Pulse until the mixture is well combined but still coarse. Set aside.

Bring a large pot of salted water to a boil. Add the pasta, stir, and cook according to the package directions, stirring occasionally, until al dente. Drain and transfer to a serving bowl. Add the cauliflower pesto and Parmesan and toss to combine. Serve right away.

wine pairing

Cauliflower has a highly adaptable flavor well suited to both white and red wine. For this dish, try a crisp Italian white from Piemonte, a Soave from the Veneto region, or even a brisk Chianti.

CHAPTER FIVE

MAIN COURSES

Be my every night dinner date

Lemongrass Shrimp Skewers

The lemongrass skewers impart a subtle lemon flavor to these Southeast Asian–inspired shrimp. Serve with steamed jasmine rice and a simple salad of sliced cucumbers tossed with a dressing of rice vinegar, Asian sesame oil, and a pinch of salt and sugar.

SERVES 6

36 large shrimp

2 Tbsp fresh lime juice

1 Tbsp Asian fish sauce

1 Tbsp brown sugar

1 small red chile, seeded and finely chopped

1 Tbsp finely chopped peeled lemongrass (white part only), plus 12 stalks to use as skewers (optional)

Fresh cilantro sprigs for garnish (optional)

Peel the shrimp, leaving the tail segments intact, and devein.

In a small bowl, whisk together the lime juice, fish sauce, brown sugar, chile, and finely chopped lemongrass. Put the marinade in a resealable plastic bag and add the shrimp. Seal and massage to coat the shrimp. Marinate for 30 minutes.

If making lemongrass skewers, remove the tough outer leaves of the stalks and trim to 6-inch (15-cm) lengths (or use 6-inch/15-cm bamboo skewers). Soak the skewers in cold water for 30 minutes.

Prepare a charcoal or gas grill for direct grilling over medium-high heat. Brush and oil the grill grate. Thread 3 shrimp onto each skewer. Place the skewers on the grill and cook, turning once, until charred in spots, 2–3 minutes total. Garnish with cilantro, if using, and serve.

natural skewers

Shrimp skewered with whole stalks
of lemongrass makes a lovely
presentation. Pierce the shrimp with
a regular skewer before attempting
to thread them onto the lemongrass.

Braised Halibut with Summer Vegetables & Orzo

The success of this one-pot meal depends on finding sea-fresh fish, flavorful tomatoes, and sweet, tender corn. To strip kernels from an ear of corn, stand the ear upright on its stem end in a wide bowl and use a sharp knife to cut downward to shear off the kernels at their base.

SERVES 4

2 lb (1 kg) heirloom tomatoes

2 Tbsp extra-virgin olive oil

1 Tbsp balsamic vinegar

3 cloves garlic, thinly sliced

Salt and freshly ground pepper

½ lb (250 g) orzo

1¼ lb (625 g) halibut fillet

½ lb (250 g) zucchini

1 cup fresh corn kernels

10 fresh basil leaves, coarsely chopped

Core the tomatoes and cut them into 1-inch (2.5-cm) chunks, reserving any juices. Put the tomatoes and their juices in a bowl and stir in the olive oil, vinegar, garlic, ½ teaspoon salt, and a few grinds of pepper. Marinate at room temperature for 30 minutes.

Bring a large pot of salted water to a boil. Add the orzo, stir, and cook, stirring occasionally, according to the package directions. Drain, rinse in cold water, and set aside.

Remove any skin from the halibut fillet and cut into 4 portions. Halve the zucchini lengthwise and cut into half-moons ⅛ inch (3 mm) thick.

In a large, deep frying pan over medium-high heat, combine the tomato mixture and the accumulated juices with ¼ cup (2 fl oz/60 ml) water and bring to a boil. Add the fish and zucchini. Reduce the heat to a gentle simmer, cover, and cook for 5 minutes. Stir in the corn and continue to cook, covered, until the fish is opaque but still moist in the center, about 5 minutes longer. Stir in the orzo and cook until heated through.

Season to taste with salt and pepper. Garnish with the basil and serve.

Sea Bass in Parchment with Salsa Verde

A robust, vivid green salsa infuses the sea bass with the tangy flavor of nutrient-packed tomatillos and spicy jalapeños. Accompany the fish with steamed brown rice or whole-wheat couscous. Any leftover salsa can be used for dressing grilled meat, fish, or poultry.

SERVES 6

6 sea bass fillets, each 5–6 oz (155–185 g) and about ¾ inch (2 cm) thick, skinned

Salt

½ lb (250 g) tomatillos, husked, rinsed, and coarsely chopped

2 bunches fresh cilantro, large stems removed, coarsely chopped

1 bunch fresh flat-leaf parsley, large stems removed, coarsely chopped

3 fresh mint sprigs, coarsely chopped

3 jalapeño chiles, coarsely chopped

5 cloves garlic, coarsely chopped

¼ white onion, coarsely chopped

¾ cup (6 fl oz/180 ml) dry white wine

⅓ cup (3 fl oz/80 ml) extra-virgin olive oil

Preheat the oven to 450°F (230°C). Sprinkle the fish on both sides with salt.

In a blender, combine the tomatillos, cilantro, parsley, mint, jalapeños, garlic, onion, and wine and blend until very smooth and thick. Season to taste with salt.

Cut 6 pieces of parchment paper, each about 12 by 18 inches (30 by 45 cm). Lay the pieces on a work surface. Brush the center of each sheet with some of the olive oil. Spoon 3 tablespoons of the sauce slightly off center on one half of each sheet, place a fillet on top of the sauce, and rub the fish generously with the remaining oil, dividing it evenly. Cover each fillet with another ½ cup (4 fl oz/125 ml) of the sauce, leaving an uncovered border at the edge of the parchment. Fold the parchment in half over the fish by bringing the short sides together and folding them over the fillet to seal. Fold in the ends so that none of the juices or steam can escape.

Place the packets on a baking sheet and place in the oven. Bake until the paper begins to brown and puff, 10–15 minutes. Remove from the oven and let stand for 5 minutes.

Place the packets on warmed plates. Carefully slit an X in the top of each packet to let the steam escape, and serve.

honey &
jalapeño

soy sauce

white miso
& sake

ginger

shallot

spiced
mayonnaise

limes

chives

Glazed Salmon Four Ways

Grilled salmon is best when seared on the outside but still moist and bright pink in the center. Glazing lends fillets a sweet and crisp exterior. If the fillets begin to overcook, finish cooking on a cooler area of the grill.

grilled salmon

4 skin-on wild salmon fillets, each about ¼ lb (125 g) and 1 inch (2.5 cm) thick, pin bones removed

Glaze of choice (at right)

Prepare a charcoal or gas grill for direct grilling over medium-high heat. Brush and oil the grill grate. (Alternatively, preheat a stove-top grill pan over medium-high heat.)

Marinate and/or glaze the fillets according to your glaze of choice.

To grill the salmon, place the fillets, skin side down, over the hottest part of the fire or in the grill pan and cook, turning once, until etched with grill marks and caramelized on both sides but still rosy pink and moist in the center, 4–6 minutes total. Serve hot.

SERVES 4

white miso
+
sake

6 Tbsp (3 oz/90 g) white miso
¼ cup (2 fl oz/60 ml) sake or mirin
3 Tbsp light agave syrup or honey
1 Tbsp firmly packed light brown sugar
1 Tbsp soy sauce
Salt and freshly ground pepper

In a small saucepan over medium-low heat, whisk together the miso, sake, agave syrup, brown sugar, and soy sauce until the sugar dissolves. Cook until slightly reduced, 3–4 minutes. Season with salt and pepper. Let cool. Brush the fillets on both sides with the glaze and grill as directed.

honey
+
jalapeño

⅓ cup (2½ fl oz/75 ml) lime juice
2 Tbsp olive oil
1½ tsp *each* minced jalapeño chile and minced fresh garlic
½ tsp grated lime zest
3 Tbsp honey

Mix the lime juice, olive oil, jalapeño, garlic, and lime zest in a shallow dish. Add the fillets and turn to coat. Cover and refrigerate for 2 hours. Remove from the refrigerator 30 minutes before grilling. Remove from the marinade. Boil the marinade in a small saucepan over high heat until reduced by half, then stir in the honey. Grill as directed. Brush with the marinade before serving.

mustard
+
soy sauce

¼ cup (2 oz/60 g) Dijon mustard
¼ cup (2 fl oz/60 ml) soy sauce
2 Tbsp firmly packed dark brown sugar
1 small clove garlic, minced
Pinch of ground cloves

Mix all the ingredients in a shallow dish. Add the fillets and turn to coat. Cover and refrigerate for at least 45 minutes. Remove from the refrigerator 15 minutes before grilling. Remove the fillets from the marinade and grill as directed.

mayonnaise
+
spices

1 Tbsp mayonnaise
1 tsp ground cumin
½ tsp *each* ground coriander, ground cinnamon, and cayenne pepper
Salt and freshly ground black pepper

Brush the fillets on all sides with the mayonnaise. Mix the cumin, coriander, cinnamon, and cayenne in a small cup and sprinkle over the mayonnaise. Grill the fillets as directed. Season to taste with salt and pepper.

Mussels Steamed in Belgian Ale, Shallots & Herbs

You'll find many types of Belgian ale on the market. For this recipe, which calls for steaming mussels in ale with aromatics, use a mild, not-too-bitter type. Don't skimp on the amount of bread you put on the table. You will both want to swab up every bit of the delicious sauce.

MAIN COURSES

SERVES 2

2 Tbsp butter

¼ cup (1 oz/30 g) finely chopped shallots

1 clove garlic, minced

½ tsp chopped fresh thyme

¾ cup (6 fl oz/180 ml) Belgian ale

1 lb (500 g) mussels, scrubbed well and beards removed

1½ tsp Dijon mustard

2 Tbsp chopped fresh flat-leaf parsley

Salt and freshly ground pepper

Crusty bread for serving

In a wide pot over medium-high heat, melt the butter. Add the shallots and sauté until soft, about 4 minutes. Add the garlic and thyme and cook for 1 minute longer.

Add the ale and bring just to a boil.

Add the mussels, cover, and cook, stirring occasionally, until the mussels open, 6–8 minutes. As they open, using a slotted spoon, transfer them to a warmed serving bowl. Discard any mussels that fail to open after 8 minutes.

Remove the pot from the heat and whisk in the mustard and parsley. Season to taste with salt and pepper. Pour the sauce over the mussels and serve with crusty bread.

Roasted Crab with Potatoes, Garlic & Fennel

This crab dish, with its buttery sauce of potatoes, garlic, and fennel, is gloriously messy. Have plenty of damp, lemon-spritzed cloth napkins on hand for dirty fingers, and a large bowl for the shells. Oyster or crab forks are a help when it comes to extracting the meat.

SERVES 2

1 lemon, cut into wedges

Kosher salt

2 live Dungeness crabs, about 1½ lb (750 g) each, or 4 blue crabs

2 fennel bulbs with stems and fronds

Olive oil for tossing

4 or 5 small new potatoes, boiled until tender and cut in half

½ cup (4 oz/125 g) unsalted butter

Cloves of 1 head garlic, minced

¼ cup (2 fl oz/60 ml) Pernod

cleaning & cracking

To clean a cooked crab, fold back the tail flap (or apron), twist off, and discard. Holding the crab with the top shell in one hand, grasp the bottom shell at the point where the apron was removed. Pull the top shell away from the body of the crab and discard. Discard the crab's internal organs, mouth, and appendages at the front, then rinse. Remove and discard the gills, which are the white feather-shaped pieces above the legs on both sides of the body. Use a nutcracker to crack the shells on the legs.

Bring a large stockpot of water to a boil and add half of the lemon wedges and ¼ cup (2 oz/60 g) salt. Cook the crabs one at a time, adding them head first and cooking for 4 minutes each, or 1 minute for blue crabs. Drain the crabs, let them cool, then clean and crack them (see note at left). Break the bodies in half and set aside.

Preheat the oven to 425°F (220°C). Trim the stems and fronds from the fennel bulbs, reserving a handful of fresh fronds (if the fronds do not look fresh, discard them). Mince enough fronds to measure about 2 tablespoons and set aside. Cut the fennel bulbs in quarters. Toss the fennel with olive oil and a pinch of salt. In a medium sauté pan over medium heat, cook the fennel quarters until they begin to turn golden brown, about 5 minutes per side. Transfer the fennel to a large roasting pan and stir in the potato pieces and crab halves.

In a small saucepan over low heat, melt the butter, add the garlic, stir, and cook for 5 minutes. Pour the butter mixture over the crab, potatoes, and fennel. Roast until the edges of the crab just begin to turn golden brown, 5–6 minutes, or 3–4 minutes for blue crabs. Arrange the crab, potatoes, and fennel on a serving platter.

Set the roasting pan with its juices and garlic on 1 or 2 burners over very low heat. Pour the Pernod into the pan, stir to combine, and cook about 1 minute. Pour the crab sauce over the crab and vegetables, garnish with the reserved minced fennel fronds, if using, and the remaining lemon wedges, and serve.

galbi house fare

In Korea, flanken-cut short ribs (known as *galbi*)
are traditionally served in "galbi houses," where
the meat is often cooked—usually by the customers
themselves—on grills set into the tables.

Korean Short Ribs

This restaurant classic is infused with plenty of sweet, salty, hot, and tangy flavors. When shopping, keep in mind that Korean-cut short ribs (thin slices cut across the ribs) are the same as flanken-cut ribs. An overnight marinade and a lightly charring 10 minutes on the grill result in an extremely flavorful dish.

SERVES 6

FOR THE MARINADE

½ cup (4 fl oz/125 ml) soy sauce, preferably low-sodium

¼ cup (2 oz/60 g) firmly packed light brown sugar

2 Tbsp rice vinegar

2 Tbsp Asian sesame oil

2 Tbsp minced garlic

1 Tbsp peeled and finely chopped fresh ginger

1 Tbsp ketchup

1 tsp red pepper flakes

5 lb (2.5 kg) flanken-cut beef short ribs, prepared by your butcher

FOR THE ASIAN-STYLE BBQ SAUCE

¼ cup (2 fl oz/60 ml) hoisin sauce

¼ cup (2 fl oz/60 ml) sweet-hot pepper sauce

2 Tbsp mirin

1 Tbsp Asian sesame oil

To make the marinade, in a large bowl, combine the soy sauce, sugar, vinegar, sesame oil, garlic, ginger, ketchup, and red pepper flakes and whisk to dissolve the sugar.

Place the ribs in a large resealable plastic bag and pour in the marinade. Seal the bag, massage the marinade around the ribs, and refrigerate in the bag overnight. Be sure to turn the bag over several times while the ribs are marinating.

Prepare a charcoal or gas grill for direct grilling over high heat. Brush and oil the grill grate.

While the grill is heating, make the BBQ sauce: In a bowl, whisk together the hoisin, pepper sauce, mirin, sesame oil, and ¼ cup (2 fl oz/60 ml) water. Taste and adjust the seasoning.

Remove the ribs from the marinade and discard the marinade. Pat the ribs dry with paper towels. Place the ribs over the hottest part of the fire and cook, turning once, until medium, 6–8 minutes total. During the last 2 minutes of cooking, brush the ribs with some of the BBQ sauce.

Transfer the ribs to a platter and let rest for 5–10 minutes. Serve with the remaining BBQ sauce at the table.

HEALTHY AND HOMEMADE

Making meals in your own kitchen means more time to
connect with your partner—and better-tasting,
more wholesome food. When you prepare dishes
at home, you can easily incorporate fresh vegetables or
focus on healthy cooking methods like grilling
and roasting. You can plan menus that rely on
what's fresh and seasonal at local farmers' markets,
skipping processed foods in favor of organic produce,
sustainably farmed meat and seafood, and whole grains.
When you make smart choices and set aside
time to cook from scratch together, you'll establish
delicious and healthy habits that last a lifetime.

Bacon-Wrapped Filets Mignons

Filet mignon, aka the King of Steak, is the center-cut portion of a beef filet and among the most tender cuts of beef. In this over-the-top preparation, the juicy medallions are enrobed in crisp slices of bacon, enhancing the filets with their smoky flavor and salty character.

SERVES 4

Simple Béarnaise Sauce (see 248), optional

8 slices thick-cut applewood–smoked bacon

4 filets mignons, each about 10 oz (315 g) and 1½ inches (4 cm) thick

Salt and freshly ground pepper

Make the Béarnaise sauce, if using. Keep warm.

Bring a saucepan half full of water to a boil. Add the bacon, reduce the heat to medium, and cook for 5 minutes. Using a slotted spoon, transfer the bacon to paper towels to drain. Discard the water.

Remove the steaks from the refrigerator at least 30 minutes before grilling. When the bacon is cool enough to handle, wrap 2 slices around the edge of each steak, then tie in place with kitchen string, snipping off any excess string. Place the steaks on a platter and brush on both sides with oil. Season the steaks on both sides with salt and pepper.

Prepare a charcoal or gas grill for direct grilling over high heat. Brush and oil the grill grate.

Place the steaks over the hottest part of the fire and cook for 4 minutes. Using tongs or a wide spatula, rotate each steak a quarter turn (90 degrees), cook 2 minutes longer, then turn and cook for an additional 6 minutes until the bacon is crisp and the steak is medium-rare. An instant-read thermometer inserted horizontally into the center of a steak should register 135°F (57°C). To cook the steaks to medium, move the steaks to a cool spot along the edge of the charcoal grill and turn down the burners on a gas grill to medium.

Transfer the steaks to warmed plates and let rest for 5–10 minutes. Snip and remove the strings and spoon the warm sauce over the steaks.

Spicy Ginger Beef & Bok Choy

Pop the flank steak into the freezer for 30 minutes, and it will be easier to slice paper-thin. You could also make the dish a vegetarian one by replacing the meat with thin slices of extra-firm tofu. Serve this quick and hearty stir-fry atop steamed white or brown rice.

SERVES 4

2 Tbsp dry sherry

1 Tbsp soy sauce, preferably low-sodium

½ tsp Asian chile paste

1 lb (500 g) baby bok choy

1 Tbsp grapeseed or canola oil

2 cloves garlic, minced

1 Tbsp peeled and minced fresh ginger

1 lb (500 g) flank steak, thinly sliced across the grain

In a small bowl, stir together the sherry, soy sauce, and chile paste. Set aside.

Trim the stem ends from the bok choy and separate into leaves. In a wok or a large nonstick frying pan over high heat, warm ½ tablespoon of the oil. When the oil is hot, add the bok choy and cook, stirring, just until tender-crisp, about 2 minutes. Transfer to a bowl.

Add the remaining ½ tablespoon oil to the pan. When hot, add the garlic and ginger and cook, stirring often, until fragrant but not browned, about 30 seconds. Add the steak to the pan and cook, tossing and stirring, just until no longer pink, about 2 minutes.

Return the bok choy to the pan along with the sherry mixture and cook until heated through, about 1 minute. Serve hot.

Cowboy Rib Eyes

You'll want bone-in rib eyes for this recipe, and if you have a good butcher, ask for the long-bone cut, known as the cowboy or tomahawk steak. The chipotle spice paste adds tons of flavor to the beef and pairs nicely with a simple corn and tomato salad.

SERVES 4

FOR THE MUSTARD VINAIGRETTE

3 Tbsp Dijon mustard

3 Tbsp cider vinegar

Juice of ½ lemon

1 tsp chopped garlic

1 tsp chopped shallot

½ tsp sugar

¼ tsp cracked yellow mustard seeds

½ cup (4 fl oz/125 ml) extra-virgin olive oil

4 bone-in rib-eye steaks, preferably long bone, each about 1½ inches (4 cm) thick

Chipotle Spice Paste (page 249)

FOR THE CORN SALAD

Mustard Vinaigrette (above)

4 spring onions or ramps, halved

4 ears corn, preferably yellow, shucked

2 large tomatoes, sliced

1 handful green beans, trimmed and blanched

1 Tbsp *each* fresh basil leaves and fresh flat-leaf parsley leaves

To make the vinaigrette, in a blender or food processor, combine the mustard, vinegar, lemon juice, garlic, shallot, sugar, and mustard seeds and pulse briefly to mix. With the motor running, slowly drizzle in the olive oil and process until the mixture emulsifies. Set aside.

Remove the steaks from the refrigerator at least 30 minutes before grilling. Rub the spice paste over both sides of the steaks. Prepare a charcoal or gas grill for direct grilling over both high heat and medium-high heat and oil the grill grate.

To make the corn salad, brush the onions with some of the vinaigrette. (Set the remaining vinaigrette aside until ready to serve.) Place the corn and onions on the grill over the medium-high part of the fire and cook, turning often, until lightly charred all the way around and the corn kernels are tender, 1–2 minutes for the onions and 5–7 minutes for the corn. Transfer to a cutting board and let cool.

Place the steaks over the hottest part of the fire and cook for 4 minutes. Using tongs or a wide spatula, rotate each steak a quarter turn (90 degrees), cook for 3 minutes longer, then turn the steaks. Cook the steaks until well marked, 5 minutes longer for medium-rare, or until an instant-read thermometer inserted into the center of a steak away from the bone registers 135°F (57°C). To cook the steaks to medium, find a cool spot along the edge of the grill or turn down the burners on the gas grill to medium until done to your liking.

Transfer the steaks to warmed plates and let rest for 5–10 minutes. Hold each ear of corn with the stem end on the cutting board and cut off the kernels with a sharp knife. Transfer to a platter and add the onions, tomatoes, and green beans, then sprinkle the herbs over the top. Drizzle the vinaigrette over the salad. Serve the steaks with the salad on the side.

MODERN
HEIRLOOM

Coconut Milk & Curry Pork Skewers

This take on one of the most popular dishes in Southeast Asian restaurants is easy to make and universally appealing. The marinade has a hint of curry, which brightens over the hot fire of the grill.

SERVES 6

FOR THE COCONUT MILK–CURRY MARINADE

1 cup (8 fl oz/250 ml) full-fat unsweetened coconut milk

¼ cup (2 fl oz/60 ml) Asian fish sauce

4 cloves garlic, finely chopped

¼ cup (⅓ oz/10 g) chopped fresh cilantro

1 tsp curry powder

Freshly ground pepper

3 lb (1.5 kg) pork tenderloin, cut into ¾-inch (2-cm) cubes

FOR THE PEANUT SAUCE

1 can (14 fl oz/430 ml) full-fat unsweetened coconut milk

¾ cup (8 oz/250 g) unsweetened, all-natural creamy peanut butter

¾ cup (6 oz/185 g) sugar

½ cup (4 fl oz/125 ml) water

2 Tbsp apple cider vinegar

3–4 Tbsp Thai red curry paste

½ Tbsp salt

Juice of ½ lime

16–20 wood skewers

To make the marinade, in a bowl, stir together the coconut milk, fish sauce, garlic, cilantro, curry powder, and 1 teaspoon pepper. Set aside.

Place the pork in a large resealable plastic bag and pour in the marinade. Seal the bag closed, massage the marinade around the pork, and refrigerate for at least 4 hours or up to 8 hours.

Meanwhile, make the peanut sauce: In a saucepan over medium heat, combine all the ingredients except the lime juice and bring to a gentle boil. Reduce the heat to low and simmer, stirring often to prevent scorching, 3–5 minutes. Let cool and set aside. Just before serving, add the lime juice and stir to blend.

At least 30 minutes before you are ready to begin grilling, remove the pork from the refrigerator. Soak the skewers in water for 30 minutes.

Prepare a charcoal or gas grill for direct grilling over high heat. Brush and oil the grill grate.

Thread the pork pieces onto the skewers, dividing them evenly. Place the skewers on the grill and cook, turning once, until the pork is lightly grill-marked on both sides and opaque throughout but still moist, 4 minutes on each side.

Arrange the skewers on a platter and let rest for about 5 minutes before serving. Pass the peanut sauce at the table.

Classic Osso Buco
with Gremolata

In this northern Italian recipe, veal shanks are braised to a melting tenderness. The meaty shanks are traditionally served over classic, saffron-scented risotto (page 141) or creamy, cooked polenta.

SERVES 6

¾ cup (4 oz/125 g) all-purpose flour

Salt and freshly ground pepper

6 veal shanks, about 6 lb (3 kg) total weight, each about 1 inch (2.5 cm) thick

¾ cup (6 fl oz/180 ml) extra-virgin olive oil

1 yellow onion, chopped

1 carrot, diced

1 rib celery, diced

2 cloves garlic, minced

1¼ cups (12 fl oz/375 ml) dry red wine such as Barolo

1 cup (6 oz/185 g) peeled, seeded, and chopped fresh or canned tomatoes

5 cups (40 fl oz/1.25 l) beef stock

FOR THE GREMOLATA

½ cup (¾ oz/20 g) minced fresh flat-leaf parsley

Grated zest of 1 lemon

2 cloves garlic, minced

Put the flour in a wide, shallow dish and season with salt and pepper. Pat the veal shanks dry with paper towels. Lightly dust the veal shanks with the seasoned flour, shaking off the excess.

In a large, heavy frying pan over medium-high heat, warm ½ cup (4 fl oz/120 ml) of the olive oil. Working in batches if necessary to avoid crowding the pan, add the shanks to the pan and cook, turning once, until well browned on both sides, about 8 minutes total. Transfer the shanks to a plate.

Return the pan to medium heat and add the remaining ¼ cup (2 fl oz/60 ml) oil. Add the onion, carrot, celery, and garlic, and sauté until softened, 3–4 minutes. Add the wine and deglaze the pan, stirring to scrape up the browned bits from the pan bottom. Raise the heat to high and cook until the liquid has thickened and is reduced by half, 3–4 minutes. Add the tomatoes and stock and bring to a boil. Reduce the heat to low, return the veal shanks to the pan, cover, and simmer, turning occasionally, for 1 hour. Uncover and cook until the veal is tender, about 30 minutes longer.

Meanwhile, to make the gremolata, in a small bowl, stir together the parsley, lemon zest, and garlic.

Divide the veal shanks among individual plates. Spoon the pan sauce over the top, sprinkle with the gremolata, and serve.

Cuban-Style Pork Tenderloin with Mojo de Ajo

In this Cuban-inspired dish, lean, tender pork is dressed with a mojo de ajo, *or "garlic sauce," that is pleasantly tangy from citrus juice and a bit spicy from red pepper flakes. Serve with two island favorites: steamed white rice and black beans.*

SERVES 4

1 tsp sweet paprika

Salt and freshly ground pepper

2 pork tenderloins, about ¾ lb (375 g) each, silver skin removed and trimmed

2 Tbsp extra-virgin olive oil

FOR THE MOJO DE AJO

¼ cup (2 fl oz/60 ml) extra-virgin olive oil

2 cloves garlic, chopped

2 Tbsp minced fresh flat-leaf parsley

½ tsp red pepper flakes

½ cup (4 fl oz/125 ml) fresh orange juice

Salt

In a small bowl, combine the paprika, 1 teaspoon salt, and ½ teaspoon pepper. Rub the paprika mixture all over the tenderloins. Transfer to a plate, cover, and let stand for 1 hour at room temperature.

Preheat the oven to 375°F (190°C).

In a large, heavy ovenproof frying pan over high heat, warm the 2 tablespoons olive oil. When the oil is shimmering, add the tenderloins and sear on all sides, about 5 minutes total. Transfer the pan to the oven and roast the pork until an instant-read thermometer inserted into the thickest part registers 135°F (57°C) for medium, about 30 minutes, or until done to your liking. Remove the pan from the oven, transfer the pork to a carving board, and tent with aluminum foil. Let rest for 10 minutes.

Meanwhile, to make the mojo de ajo, in a small nonreactive frying pan over medium-low heat, warm the ¼ cup (2 fl oz/60 ml) olive oil. Add the garlic and cook, stirring often, until golden brown, about 4 minutes. Stir in the parsley and pepper flakes and cook for 10 seconds. Add the orange juice and simmer, swirling the pan once or twice, until slightly reduced, about 2 minutes. Season to taste with salt. Remove from the heat.

Cut each tenderloin crosswise into thick slices. Arrange the slices on a warmed platter or individual plates. Spoon the sauce over the pork and serve.

cast-iron classic

If you have a cast-iron pan, now is the time to use it.
The pan's durable, forearm-flexing iron provides
a lifetime of use and offers the perfect vehicle for
caramelizing meat to mouthwatering perfection.

Brined Pork Chops & Grilled Stone Fruit

Pork chops are a great cut for grilling, but because they can be lean, they can easily dry out. Brining them adds flavor and ensures a moist, tender result. Add a sprinkle of chopped red onion over the fruit, if you like, for a nice counterpoint to the stone fruit's sweet flavor.

SERVES 6

FOR THE BRINE

¼ cup (2 fl oz/60 ml) apple cider vinegar

¼ cup (2 oz/60 g) firmly packed brown sugar

1 tsp dried thyme

1 tsp juniper berries (optional)

⅛ tsp red pepper flakes

2 Tbsp kosher salt

1 Tbsp freshly ground black pepper

6 bone-in pork chops, each at least 1 inch (2.5 cm) thick

Olive oil for brushing

6 ripe but slightly firm plums, peaches, or nectarines, halved and pitted

¼ red onion, finely chopped (optional)

To make the brine, in a large bowl, combine 6 cups (48 fl oz/ 1.5 l) water, the vinegar, sugar, thyme, juniper berries (if using), red pepper flakes, salt, and black pepper and stir until the sugar and salt dissolve.

Place the pork chops in a large resealable plastic bag and pour in the brine. Seal the bag closed, massage the brine around the chops, and refrigerate for at least 4 hours.

Remove the chops from the refrigerator at least 30 minutes before grilling. Discard the brine, rinse the chops briefly in cold water, and pat dry with paper towels.

Prepare a charcoal or gas grill for indirect grilling over medium heat; the temperature inside the grill should be 350°–375°F (180°–190°C). Brush and oil the grill grate. For a charcoal grill, bank the lit coals on either side of the grill bed, leaving a strip in the center without heat, and place a drip pan in the center. For a gas grill, preheat the burners, then turn off 1 or more of the burners to create a cooler zone.

Place the chops over the direct-heat area and sear, turning once, until nicely grill-marked on both sides, 2–3 minutes on each side. Move the chops to the indirect-heat area, cover the grill, and cook until the chops are somewhat firm to the touch, about 15 minutes for medium, or until an instant-read thermometer inserted horizontally into the center of a chop away from the bone registers 145°F (63°C).

Transfer the chops to a platter and let rest for 10 minutes. Meanwhile, brush the cut sides of the fruit halves with oil and grill over the direct-heat area until nicely grill-marked, about 2 minutes on each side. Serve the pork chops with the grilled fruit on the side. Sprinkle red onion over the fruit, if desired.

Roast Chicken with Spice Rub

Whole roast chicken is tops when it comes to no-fuss dinners. This recipe, with its choice of herb- or spice-centric rub and simple pan sauce, is one you'll turn to again and again. Tie the chicken legs together before cooking to help the bird to cook more evenly.

SERVES 2–4

1 whole chicken, about 4 lb (2 kg)

Olive oil for rubbing

Chipotle Spice Rub or Herb-Spice Rub (page 249)

Salt and freshly ground pepper

½ cup (4 fl oz/125 ml) dry white wine

1 cup (8 fl oz/250 ml) chicken broth

Fresh lemon juice to taste

Preheat the oven to 425°F (220°C). If the giblets are in the chicken cavity, remove them and reserve for another use or discard. Remove and discard any excess fat on the chicken. Tie the legs together with kitchen string and tuck the wing tips under the shoulders.

Place the chicken, breast side up, in a roasting pan. Rub the chicken all over with oil, then sprinkle all over with the spice rub. Season well with salt and pepper. Roast the chicken until the skin is browned and an instant-read thermometer inserted in the thickest part of the thigh away from the bone registers 170°F (77°C), about 1 hour and 10 minutes (12–15 minutes per lb/500 g). Transfer the chicken to a carving board and let rest for 15 minutes.

Place the roasting pan on the stove top over medium heat and add the wine. Bring to a boil and deglaze, stirring to scrape up any browned bits on the pan bottom. Add the broth and boil until the liquid is reduced to about 1 cup (8 fl oz/250 ml), about 3 minutes. Remove from the heat. Season to taste with salt, pepper, and lemon juice, then pour into a warmed serving bowl. Cut the chicken into pieces and serve, passing the sauce at the table.

a wish come true

If you listen to the tales of old wives, don't miss the wishbone from a whole bird (located just above the breasts). Each of you take an end of the small bone and twist—big piece gets the wish.

Classic Yellow Chicken Curry

For a quicker version of this curry, substitute a cut-up rotisserie chicken for the chicken pieces and skip the searing step. Proceed with the recipe as directed, simmering the potatoes and carrots in the curry sauce until tender, about 40 minutes, then adding the rotisserie chicken during the last 10 minutes of cooking.

SERVES 4–6

2 lb (1 kg) skin-on, bone-in chicken breasts and/or thighs

2 tsp salt

2 Tbsp corn or peanut oil

1 yellow onion, chopped

1 Tbsp peeled and minced fresh ginger

3 cloves garlic, minced

1½ Tbsp curry powder

1 can (13.5 fl oz/420 ml) unsweetened coconut milk

Juice of 1 lemon

2 large boiling potatoes, peeled and cut into large cubes

2 carrots, peeled and cut into large pieces

Steamed rice for serving

Sprinkle the chicken pieces evenly with 1 teaspoon of the salt. Warm a Dutch oven or large ovenproof frying pan over high heat until very hot and add the oil. Add the chicken, skin side down, and sear until crisp and brown, 5–6 minutes. Turn the pieces and sear again, 5–6 minutes longer. Using tongs or a slotted spoon, transfer the chicken to a plate.

Preheat the oven to 325°F (165°C). Return the pan to high heat, add the onion, ginger, and garlic, and sauté until just tender, about 2 minutes. Stir in the curry powder and sauté 10 seconds longer. Add the coconut milk, ½ cup (4 fl oz/125 ml) water, the lemon juice, and the remaining 1 teaspoon salt. Bring to a boil, return the chicken pieces to the pan, and simmer for 2 minutes. Cover tightly, transfer to the oven, and cook for 30 minutes. Remove from the oven, stir in the potatoes and carrots, cover, return to the oven, and continue to cook until the potatoes and carrots are tender, about 30 minutes longer. Uncover and cook for a final 10 minutes to allow the curry to thicken. Serve with the rice.

Individual Chicken Pot Pies

Chicken pot pie is comfort food at its best. Store-bought pie dough and the meat from a cooked chicken bring these pot pies to the table in record time. Bake as many as you like and freeze the remainder: Wrap securely and freeze for up to 2 months, then bake directly from the freezer, adding several minutes to the baking time.

SERVES 6

3 Tbsp unsalted butter

1 Tbsp olive oil

½ yellow onion, chopped

2 carrots, peeled and chopped

2 cloves garlic, minced

6 white or brown mushrooms, sliced

5 fresh sage leaves, chopped

Salt and freshly ground pepper

½ cup (2½ oz/75 g) thawed frozen peas

¼ cup (1½ oz/45 g) all-purpose flour

1½ cups (12 fl oz/375 ml) low-sodium chicken broth

½ cup (4 fl oz/125 ml) dry white wine

½ cup (4 fl oz/125 ml) half-and-half

4 cups (1½ lb/750 g) cooked, cubed chicken

Double-Crust Flaky Pie Dough (page 250) or purchased pie dough for 2 full-size pies, refrigerated

Preheat the oven to 375°F (190°C).

In a large frying pan over medium-high heat, warm 1 tablespoon of the butter and the olive oil. Add the onion and the carrots and sauté until soft, about 8 minutes. Add the garlic, mushrooms, and sage and season well with salt and pepper. Cook, stirring occasionally, until the mushrooms are soft, about 4 minutes. Transfer to a large bowl and stir in the peas. Do not wipe the pan clean and keep it over medium-high heat.

Add the remaining 2 tablespoons butter to the pan. Sprinkle in the flour and cook, stirring constantly, for 1 minute. Stir in the broth, wine, and half-and-half and bring to a simmer. Cook, stirring often, until the sauce thickens, about 5 minutes. Remove from the heat, add the cooked chicken, and let cool slightly. Add to the bowl with the vegetables and stir to combine well. Season with salt and pepper and divide the mixture among six 4½-inch (11.5-cm) ramekins or other round baking dishes.

Remove the dough from the refrigerator, unwrap, and let stand for a few minutes to soften slightly. Roll each piece of dough into a round. Using the bottom of one of the baking dishes as a guide, and with the tip of a sharp knife, cut out 6 circles that are about ¼ inch (6 mm) bigger than the dish. Place a dough circle over the filling in each dish, pressing the dough onto the rim of the dishes. Crimp the edges and place the dishes on a baking sheet. Bake until the crust is golden brown, 20–25 minutes. Remove from the oven and let cool for 5 minutes, then serve.

Sautéed Chicken Breasts with Warm Tomato Salad

Cherry tomatoes, which pack a healthful punch—vitamins A, B₆, and C, and the potent antioxidant lycopene—are often employed as a garnish rather than a central ingredient. Here, as a sauté atop lean chicken breasts, they make a nutritious one-dish weeknight supper.

SERVES 4

4 boneless, skinless chicken breast halves, about 6 oz (185 g) each

Salt and freshly ground pepper

2 Tbsp olive oil

1 or 2 large shallots, minced

1 clove garlic, minced

1½ cups (9 oz/280 g) cherry and pear tomatoes, preferably a mix of colors and shapes, halved

3 Tbsp balsamic vinegar

½ cup (½ oz/15 g) packed fresh basil leaves, torn

One at a time, place the chicken breasts between 2 pieces of plastic wrap and lightly pound with a meat pounder to a thickness of about ½ inch (12 mm). Season the chicken generously on both sides with salt and pepper.

In a large nonstick frying pan over medium-high heat, warm the olive oil. Working in batches to avoid crowding, add the chicken and reduce the heat to medium. Cook, turning once, until nicely browned and opaque throughout, 4–5 minutes per side. Transfer the cooked pieces to a platter and cover with aluminum foil to keep warm.

Add the shallots and garlic to the frying pan and cook, stirring often, until softened, 3–4 minutes. Add the tomatoes and vinegar and cook, stirring often, until the tomatoes begin to soften and split, about 4 minutes. Stir in the basil and season with salt and pepper.

To serve, place a chicken breast on each of 4 warmed individual plates and spoon the warm tomato salad on top. Serve right away.

best in season

This dish is especially good in the summer months, when tomatoes are at their peak. Use the very best cherry tomatoes you can find, combining different varieties when you can get them. Sauté the ripe tomatoes quickly so they remain both firm and bright.

Grilled Ginger-Soy Chicken

The ginger lends a sweet tang to this succulent chicken dish. If ginger preserve is unavailable, use the same quantity of lemon or orange marmalade plus 1 tablespoon peeled and minced fresh ginger.

SERVES 4

FOR THE GINGER-SOY GLAZE

¼ cup (2½ oz/75 g) ginger preserve

3 Tbsp minced shallots

3 Tbsp fresh lemon juice

2 Tbsp olive oil

2 Tbsp soy sauce, preferably low-sodium

2½ lb (1.15 kg) chicken thighs and legs

Olive oil for brushing

Salt and freshly ground pepper

To make the ginger-soy glaze, in a bowl, whisk together the ginger preserve, shallots, lemon juice, olive oil, and soy sauce. Set aside.

Prepare a charcoal or gas grill for indirect grilling over medium heat; the temperature inside the grill should be 325°–350°F (160°–180°C). If using charcoal, bank the lit coals on either side of the grill bed, leaving a strip in the center without heat, and place a drip pan in the center. If using gas, preheat the burners, then turn off 1 or more of the burners to create a cooler zone. Brush and oil the grill grate.

Pat the chicken dry with paper towels. Brush all over with olive oil and season with salt and pepper. Place the chicken pieces on the grill rack over the direct-heat area and sear, turning once, for 2 minutes on each side. Move the chicken pieces to the indirect-heat area, cover the grill, and cook for 20 minutes. Brush the chicken with the glaze, cover, and continue grilling, turning and brushing with glaze every 5 minutes, until an instant-read thermometer inserted into a thigh away from the bone registers 165°F (74°C), 10-15 minutes longer.

Transfer the chicken to a platter and serve hot. Pass the remaining sauce at the table.

Cheese Soufflé

Featherlight cheese soufflé makes for an intimate evening supper. Pair it with a simply dressed butter lettuce salad and a bottle of chilled Champagne. To achieve the loftiest rise, use room-temperature egg whites and fold in the beaten whites just until no white streaks remain.

SERVES 4

2½ Tbsp unsalted butter, plus more for greasing

1 cup (4 oz/125 g) plus 2 Tbsp shredded Gruyère or Comté cheese

3 Tbsp all-purpose flour

1 cup (8 fl oz/250 ml) whole milk

4 large egg yolks

1 tsp Dijon mustard

Salt and freshly ground white pepper

Pinch of freshly grated nutmeg

5 large egg whites

Pinch of cream of tartar

1 Tbsp fine fresh or dried bread crumbs

Preheat the oven to 375°F (190°C). Butter a 6-cup (48-fl oz/1.5 l) soufflé dish and coat the bottom and sides evenly with 1 tablespoon of the cheese.

In a saucepan over medium heat, melt the butter. Add the flour and mix with a wooden spoon for 1 minute. Cook until the mixture is bubbling but still white, about 2 minutes longer. While whisking constantly, add the milk. Bring to a simmer and continue to whisk until the sauce is thick and smooth, about 2 minutes longer. Remove from the heat and let cool for 10 minutes.

Add the egg yolks one at a time to the cooled milk mixture, whisking after each addition until smooth. Add the mustard, ½ teaspoon salt, a grind or two of white pepper, and the nutmeg and whisk to combine.

In a large, clean bowl, using a large balloon whisk or an electric mixer on medium speed, whip the egg whites with a pinch of salt and cream of tartar until stiff, glossy peaks form. The peaks should stand upright on the whisk or beaters when lifted. Do not overbeat or the whites will become rough and lumpy.

Using a spatula, gently fold half of the egg whites into the milk mixture to lighten it. Gently stir in 1 cup (4 oz/125 g) of the shredded cheese and then fold in the remaining egg whites just until no white streaks remain. Scoop the egg white mixture into the prepared dish. Sprinkle the remaining 1 tablespoon cheese and the bread crumbs evenly over the top.

Bake until the soufflé is puffed and the top is browned, 30–35 minutes. Serve right away.

Cheese Fondue

With luck, you were given a fondue pot as a wedding gift, which means you can now put it to work. Don't skimp on the quality of the cheese or wine, or your fondue will suffer. Serve a simple green salad and some crisp apple slices for dipping to help temper the richness of the cheese.

SERVES 4

4–5 cloves garlic

1 bottle (24 fl oz/750 ml) dry white wine such as Sauvignon Blanc

½ tsp salt

1½ lb (750 g) Beaufort or Gruyère cheese, shredded

½ lb (250 g) Comté or Emmentaler cheese, shredded

Pinch of freshly grated nutmeg

¼ cup (2 fl oz/60 ml) kirsch

¼ tsp freshly ground pepper

1 Tbsp unsalted butter

2 day-old baguettes, cut into 1-inch (2.5-cm) cubes

4 fondue forks or other long skewers, for serving

Using a garlic press, squeeze the garlic cloves into a fondue pot. Discard the pulp that remains in the press. Pour in the wine and add the salt. Place the pot over medium-high heat and cook just until bubbles begin to appear along the edges of the pot.

Using a wooden spoon, stir in both cheeses. Cook, stirring, until the cheeses are nearly melted and the mixture turns yellow, about 10 minutes. Reduce the heat to medium-low and stir in the nutmeg and then the kirsch. Continuing to stir, add the pepper and the butter. Stir until the butter is melted.

To serve, light the fuel burner for the fondue pot according to the manufacturer's instructions. Place the hot fondue pot over the burner. Offer the bread cubes in a bowl or basket alongside. Using the fondue forks or skewers, pierce the bread cubes one at a time, dipping them into the fondue until well coated.

Roasted Vegetable, Tofu & Barley Bowl

Cooking barley is as easy as cooking rice, and the hearty flavors in this vegan-friendly bowl are an excellent reason to eat this healthful, satisfying grain more often.

SERVES 4

2 lb (1 kg) assorted baby beets, rinsed and tops trimmed to ½ inch (15 mm)

4 Tbsp (2 fl oz/60 ml) plus 2 tsp olive oil

Salt

1 lb (500 g) broccoli rabe, trimmed

2 cloves garlic, smashed

⅛ tsp red pepper flakes

4 radishes, trimmed

2 large carrots, trimmed

1 block (14 oz/440 g) firm tofu, drained, patted dry, and cut crosswise into 8 slices ½ inch (12 mm) thick

8 tsp harissa, store-bought or homemade (page 248), plus more for serving

3½ cups (5½ oz/160 g) cooked pearl barley

1 cup (5 oz/155 g) shelled fresh peas, blanched, or frozen peas, thawed

Preheat the oven to 400°F (200°C). Place the beets in a shallow baking dish, drizzle with 1 tablespoon of the olive oil, and toss to coat. Cover the pan tightly with aluminum foil and bake until the beets are tender when pierced with knife, about 40 minutes. Do not turn off the oven. Place the dish on a wire rack, uncover, and let cool, then peel off the skins. Halve or quarter the beets and season with salt.

On a baking sheet, toss the broccoli rabe and garlic with 2 tablespoons of the olive oil and season with salt and the red pepper flakes. Spread in one layer and bake until the broccoli rabe is bright green and the stems are tender when pierced with the tip of a sharp knife, about 10 minutes. Discard the garlic. Cover the baking sheet lightly with foil to keep warm.

Using a mandoline or a vegetable peeler, cut the radishes and carrots lengthwise into thin slices. Place the radishes on a plate and set aside. In a large nonstick frying pan over medium heat, warm the 2 teaspoons olive oil with 1 tablespoon of water. Add the carrots and season lightly with salt. Cook, covered, until crisp-tender, about 5 minutes. Transfer to the plate with the radishes and set aside. Wipe the skillet clean with a paper towel.

Warm the remaining 1 tablespoon olive oil in the frying pan over medium-high heat. Working in batches if necessary, add the tofu without crowding and cook, turning once, until golden on the outside and heated through, 4–6 minutes total. Spread about 1 teaspoon harissa over each slice.

Divide the barley and peas among 4 wide, shallow bowls. Arrange the beets, broccoli rabe, radishes, carrots, and tofu slices over the top and serve, passing extra harissa at the table.

seasonal bowls

These healthful bowls are easy to vary according to whatever fresh produce is in season. Use a range of flavors, textures, and shapes for the most satisfying bowl.

CHAPTER SIX

SIDE DISHES

Our love story is my favorite

Grilled Asparagus with Orange, Endive & Fresh Fava Beans

If it's still too cold to grill outdoors, you can cook this springtime dish on a stove-top grill pan with similar results. You can switch up the ingredients too, substituting English peas for the fava beans or fennel for the endive. Try it alongside grilled fish or other light preparation.

SERVES 4

Salt and freshly ground pepper

3 lb fresh fava beans, pods removed

1 lb slender asparagus, ends trimmed

2 heads Belgian endive, sliced lengthwise ⅛ inch (3 mm) thick

1 orange

½ cup (4 fl oz/125 ml) extra-virgin olive oil

½ cup (½ oz/15 g) fresh mint leaves

Bring a large pot of salted water to a boil. Prepare a large bowl of ice water.

Blanch the fava beans in boiling water for 1 minute. Drain and transfer to the bowl of ice water. When the beans are cool, use your fingers to peel off the skins. Set the fava beans aside.

Prepare a charcoal or gas grill for direct grilling over high heat. Brush and oil the grill grate. Place the asparagus and endive directly on the grill rack, or use a grill screen. Grill, turning occasionally, until evenly charred, 2–3 minutes. Transfer to a serving platter and season well with salt and pepper.

Using a zester, zest the orange over a bowl. Using a sharp knife, cut a slice off both ends of the orange to reveal the flesh. Stand the orange upright on a cutting board and cut downward to remove the peel and white pith. Holding the orange in one hand over the bowl, cut along both sides of each segment to release it from the membrane, letting the segments and juice drop into the bowl. Remove any seeds. Add the olive oil to the bowl and whisk until blended. Season to taste with salt and pepper.

Scatter the fava beans and mint over the grilled vegetables. Drizzle with the orange dressing and serve.

cooking note

Fresh vegetables in season are best
cooked until tender, but still crisp.
Watch carefully and remove them
from the heat when still slightly firm.

Broccoli Rabe with Almond Pesto

Broccoli rabe, with its slender stalks, small florets, and slightly bitter flavor, is a favorite of the Italian kitchen. Be sure to trim away any thick stems to ensure the green is tender when served. This brightly flavored dish is a nice accompaniment to panfried chops or cutlets.

SERVES 4

Salt

½ lb (250 g) broccoli rabe, trimmed

1 large clove garlic

1 cup (1 oz/30 g) lightly packed fresh flat-leaf parsley leaves

⅓ cup (3 fl oz/80 ml) extra-virgin olive oil

⅓ cup (2 oz/60 g) blanched almonds, toasted and coarsely chopped

Prepare a large bowl of ice water. Bring a large saucepan of salted water to a boil. Add the broccoli rabe and cook for 3 minutes. Drain and immediately plunge the broccoli rabe into the ice water. Drain and set aside.

In a food processor or blender, combine the garlic, parsley, and ½ teaspoon salt and process until the parsley is finely chopped. With the machine running, add the olive oil in a slow, steady stream and process until a purée forms. Add the almonds and pulse until finely chopped and the pesto is a uniform coarse purée.

Place the broccoli rabe in a large bowl and pat dry with paper towels if needed. Add the pesto and toss to coat evenly. Arrange the broccoli rabe on a serving platter and serve at room temperature.

Quinoa Pilaf with Apricots & Almonds

This citrus-scented pilaf pairs well with grilled or roasted meats or makes a satisfying light main course for vegetarians. Quinoa is an easy-to-cook nutritional powerhouse, so always keep some in your pantry for when you need a tasty whole-grain side dish.

SERVES 4

½ cup (4 fl oz/125 ml) fresh orange juice

⅛ tsp ground turmeric

Salt and freshly ground pepper

1 cup (8 oz/250 g) quinoa, rinsed

⅓ cup (2 oz/60 g) slivered almonds

⅓ cup (2 oz/60 g) dried apricots, thinly sliced

1 Tbsp extra-virgin olive oil

1 Tbsp fresh lemon juice

Grated zest of 1 orange

In a saucepan over high heat, combine the orange juice, turmeric, ⅛ teaspoon salt, and 1 cup (8 fl oz/250 ml) water. Bring to a boil. Add the quinoa, cover, and reduce the heat to maintain a gentle simmer. Simmer until the liquid is absorbed, about 20 minutes.

Meanwhile, preheat the oven to 350°F (180°C). Spread the almonds on a baking sheet and toast until lightly browned and fragrant, about 10 minutes. Immediately pour onto a plate to cool.

Fluff the quinoa with a fork to separate the grains. Stir in the almonds, apricots, olive oil, lemon juice, and orange zest. Season to taste with salt and pepper and serve.

Roasted Cauliflower with Chile, Meyer Lemon & Currants

Mild-tasting cauliflower shines when partnered with robustly flavored ingredients. You can prepare the cauliflower for roasting the day before, then combine it with the seasonings just before it goes in the oven. Any leftovers are good served at room temperature for an easy lunch.

SERVES 4–6

1 large cauliflower, about 2 lb (1 kg)

3 Tbsp olive oil

1 Tbsp hot Calabrian chile spread (available at specialty-food stores or online) or other chile paste

1 small Meyer lemon, quartered and cut crosswise into thin wedges

Salt

1½ Tbsp currants

2 Tbsp pine nuts, lightly toasted

Fresh dill sprigs for garnish (optional)

Preheat the oven to 450°F (230°C). Separate the cauliflower into florets and cut the stem into bite-size pieces, discarding any tough parts.

In a bowl, combine the cauliflower, olive oil, chile spread, lemon, and ½ teaspoon salt and toss to coat. Spread in a single layer on a rimmed baking sheet and roast for 10 minutes. Stir well and continue to roast until the cauliflower is tender and browned in spots, 5–10 minutes longer. Remove from the oven, sprinkle the currants on top, and toss gently to combine.

Transfer the cauliflower to a serving platter and sprinkle with the pine nuts. Garnish with dill sprigs, if desired. Serve hot or warm.

Israeli Couscous with Mint, Feta & Roasted Squash

Israeli couscous is larger—about the size of small pearls, thus its other name, pearl couscous—and denser than North African couscous. The use of acorn squash makes this simple side dish ideal for the autumn dinner table. If you like, exchange the acorn squash for kabocha.

SERVES 8

1 Tbsp chopped fresh sage

Salt

1 tsp ground cinnamon

1 tsp chili powder

1 tsp freshly ground pepper

2 acorn squash, about 2½ lb (1.25 kg) total weight

Extra-virgin olive oil for brushing and drizzling

2 cups (12 oz/375 g) Israeli couscous

6 oz (185 g) feta cheese, crumbled

¾ cup (3 oz/90 g) toasted almonds

¼ cup (¼ oz/7 g) minced fresh mint, plus sprigs for garnish

Preheat the oven to 350°F (180°C). In a small bowl, combine the sage, 1 teaspoon salt, the cinnamon, chili powder, and pepper and mix well.

Cut the squash crosswise into rings about 1 inch (2.5 cm) thick and discard the seeds. Brush the cut sides with olive oil, then rub with the sage mixture. Arrange the rings on a baking sheet. Roast until lightly browned and easily pierced with a knife, about 1 hour. Peel and cut each ring into 4 sections.

Place the couscous in a colander and rinse with cold water. Cook according to the package directions. Transfer the cooked couscous to a warmed platter. Drizzle with a little olive oil and fluff gently to separate the grains. Season to taste with salt.

To serve, sprinkle the couscous with the feta, almonds, and minced mint. Turn gently to distribute the ingredients, then fold in the squash and garnish with the mint sprigs. Serve warm or at room temperature.

modern versatility

This wholesome dish is equally at home
served alongside roast chicken (page 170),
grilled salmon (page 153), or brined pork
chops (page 169), or paired with braised
tofu for a meat-free main course.

Lentils with Shallots & Prosciutto

The small amount of prosciutto in this dish adds big flavor without a lot of extra fat. Lean bacon or pancetta can be used the same way to flavor lentils or other naturally bland legumes. Serve this protein-rich side dish alongside grilled salmon (page 153).

SERVES 4

¾ cup (5 oz/155 g) brown lentils, rinsed

1 Tbsp olive oil

¾ cup (4 oz/125 g) finely chopped fennel bulb, plus chopped fronds for garnish

¼ cup (1 oz/30 g) finely chopped shallots

2 Tbsp sherry vinegar

2 oz (60 g) prosciutto, cut into ribbons

Salt and freshly ground pepper

In a saucepan over medium-high heat, combine the lentils with water to cover by 2 inches (5 cm) and bring to a boil. Reduce the heat to medium-low, cover, and simmer gently until the lentils are tender but firm to the bite, about 20 minutes. Scoop out ¼ cup (2 fl oz/ 60 ml) of the cooking water and reserve. Drain the lentils thoroughly in a colander, then return to the saucepan.

In a frying pan over medium-high heat, warm the olive oil. Add the finely chopped fennel and shallots and cook, stirring often, until golden, about 8 minutes. Scrape the contents of the frying pan into the saucepan with the lentils.

Add the vinegar and reserved cooking water to the frying pan, bring to a boil, and cook until the liquid is reduced by half, about 3 minutes. Add the hot liquid to the lentils and stir in the prosciutto. Season to taste with salt and pepper.

Transfer the lentils to a serving bowl or platter, sprinkle with the fennel fronds, and serve.

Sautéed Garden Peas with Basil & Pecorino

Rich in vitamins K and C, English peas and sugar snap peas are ideal candidates for weeknight menus, as they can be prepped and cooked quickly and easily. For a different but equally satisfying flavor, substitute fresh mint leaves for the basil.

SERVES 4

1 Tbsp unsalted butter

1 Tbsp olive oil

½ lb (250 g) sugar snap peas, strings removed

1 lb (500 g) English peas, shelled

Salt and freshly ground pepper

1 lemon

Leaves from 4 basil sprigs, torn

1 piece (about 1 oz/30 g) pecorino-romano cheese

In a large frying pan over medium heat, melt the butter in the olive oil. Add the snap peas and English peas. Pour in ¼ cup (2 fl oz/60 ml) water and add a pinch of salt. Cover and cook for 2 minutes. Uncover and cook, stirring occasionally, until the water has evaporated and the peas are crisp-tender and still bright green, about 2 minutes longer.

Finely grate 2 teaspoons zest from the lemon, then halve the lemon. Remove the pan from the heat and squeeze the juice from 1 lemon half over the peas (reserve the remaining half for another use). Add the lemon zest and basil and season with a pinch each of salt and pepper. Grate the cheese over the top to taste and stir to mix well.

Transfer the peas to a warmed serving dish and serve.

garlic

thyme

shallots

butter

chives

chervil

Mashed Potatoes Five Ways

A ricer makes quick work of mashing potatoes. Just feed the cooked potatoes into the hopper, depress the plunger, and light, perfectly smooth mashed potatoes emerge from the bottom. A mixer or masher works well too.

mashed potatoes

3 lb (1.5 kg) russet potatoes, peeled and cut into chunks

Salt and freshly ground white pepper

½ cup (4 oz/125 g) unsalted butter, at room temperature

About ½ cup (4 fl oz/125 ml) whole milk, warmed

3 Tbsp minced fresh chives (optional)

In a large saucepan over high heat, combine the potatoes with salted water to cover and bring to a boil. Reduce the heat to medium-low and simmer until the potatoes are tender when pierced with a knife, about 20 minutes. Drain well. Return the potatoes to the pan and stir over medium-low heat for 2 minutes to evaporate the excess moisture.

Press the warm potatoes through a ricer into a large bowl or beat the potatoes in the pot with a handheld mixer on high speed, being careful not to overbeat them. Cut the butter into slices and scatter over the potatoes. Whisk in the butter and enough warm milk to produce the desired texture. Mix in the chives, if using, and season to taste with salt and white pepper.

Transfer to a warmed serving bowl and serve right away.

SERVES 6

new potatoes + mascarpone

Substitute new potatoes for the russet potatoes. Add ¼ cup (2 oz/60 g) mascarpone cheese to the cooked potatoes before mashing and reduce the milk to ¼ cup (2 fl oz/60 ml). Sprinkle with the chives, or substitute with 1 tablespoon minced fresh chervil, if you wish.

pecan + sweet potato

Substitute sweet potatoes for the russet potatoes. Before serving, sauté ⅓ cup (1½ oz/40 g) chopped pecans in 2 tablespoons butter over medium-low heat until lightly toasted, about 3 minutes, then pour over the top. Omit the chives.

lemon + thyme

In a small bowl, mix 2 tablespoons of the butter with 1 teaspoon minced fresh thyme and a scant ¼ teaspoon minced lemon zest. Add the flavored butter with the remaining 6 tablespoons plain butter before whisking. Omit the chives, adding a sprinkling of extra minced lemon zest and fresh thyme leaves over the mashed potatoes.

Yukon gold + garlic

Substitute Yukon gold potatoes for the russet potatoes. While they are cooking, melt 2 tablespoons butter in a small saucepan over low heat. Add 2 tablespoons minced garlic to the pan and sauté until softened, about 2 minutes. Add to the mashed potatoes and stir until blended. Add the chives, if you wish. (For onion flavor, use 3 tablespoons butter and sauté 2 tablespoons minced shallots for 2 minutes before adding the garlic.)

Scalloped Potatoes with Leeks & Gruyère

This updated version of the traditional side dish standby combines nutty Gruyère, rich cream, and tender leeks in a dish that's classy enough—and generous enough—for company. Leftovers can be tightly covered and reheated in a 350°F (180°C) oven.

SERVES 8

2 Tbsp unsalted butter, plus more for greasing

3 cups (12 oz/375 g) chopped leeks, including tender green tops

Salt and freshly ground pepper

3¾ lb (1.85 kg) russet potatoes, peeled and thinly sliced

2 cups (8 oz/250 g) shredded Gruyère cheese

3 cups (24 fl oz/750 ml) heavy cream

classic variation

Omit the butter and leeks. Substitute sharp white Cheddar for the Gruyère and whole milk for the cream. As you add the potatoes, sprinkle each interior layer with 1 tablespoon all-purpose flour when you add the salt mixture.

Preheat the oven to 350°F (180°C). Generously butter a 9-by-13-inch (23-by-33-cm) baking dish.

In a large frying pan over medium heat, melt the 2 tablespoons butter. Add the leeks and cook, stirring occasionally, until tender, about 7 minutes. Remove from the heat.

In a small bowl, mix together 2 teaspoons salt and ½ teaspoon pepper. Spread one-third of the potatoes in an even layer in the prepared dish and season with about one-fourth of the salt mixture. Top with one-third of the Gruyère and half of the leeks and season with about one-third of the remaining salt mixture. Top with half of the remaining potato slices, half of the remaining Gruyère, and the rest of the leeks, seasoning with half of the remaining salt mixture. Finish with the remaining potatoes and Gruyère and season with the remaining salt mixture.

In a small saucepan over medium-high heat, bring the cream to a simmer. Pour the hot cream over the potatoes. Cover the dish tightly with aluminum foil and place on a baking sheet. Bake for 1 hour.

Remove the foil and continue to bake until the potatoes are tender, coated with a creamy sauce, and golden brown on top, about 30 minutes. Let stand for about 5 minutes before serving.

Butternut Squash & Pears with Rosemary

Winter squash can take a long time to cook, which keeps most varieties off weeknight menus. But in this recipe, butternut squash, which is packed with vitamins A, C, and potassium, is thinly sliced, so it's ready to eat in no more than 15 minutes.

SERVES 4

1 Bosc pear

1 Tbsp grapeseed or canola oil

½ small butternut squash, about ¾ lb (375 g), peeled, seeded, and thinly sliced

Salt

1 Tbsp finely chopped fresh rosemary

Pinch of cayenne pepper

½ cup (4 fl oz/125 ml) apple juice

Halve and core the pear and cut lengthwise into thin slices.

In a frying pan over medium-high heat, warm the oil. Add the squash and sprinkle with 1 teaspoon salt. Cook, stirring often, until the squash is browned on the edges and begins to soften, about 5 minutes.

Add the pear, rosemary, cayenne, and apple juice and cook until the liquid evaporates and the squash is tender, 6–8 minutes longer.

Transfer to a serving bowl. Serve hot, warm, or at room temperature.

Roasted Carrots with Fennel, Pistachios & Honey Vinaigrette

Here, carrots are treated to a fennel-infused olive oil, roasted, and then glazed with honey and vinegar when they are piping hot. Purple, gold, and red rainbow carrots make for a beautiful presentation, but if you can't find them, conventional orange carrots will do.

SERVES 4

2 tsp fennel seeds, toasted and coarsely ground

3 Tbsp extra-virgin olive oil

1 lb (500 g) rainbow carrots, trimmed

Salt and freshly ground pepper

1 Tbsp honey

2 tsp white balsamic vinegar

1 Tbsp crushed unsalted roasted pistachios

Place the fennel seeds in a bowl and stir in the olive oil. Let steep for 30 minutes.

Preheat the oven to 400°F (200°C). Place the carrots on a rimmed baking sheet and drizzle the fennel-infused oil over them. Season with salt and pepper. Roll the carrots around to coat completely with the oil, then arrange in a single layer. Roast until the carrots are tender and lightly browned, 20–25 minutes. Keep the oven on.

In a small bowl, whisk together the honey and vinegar.

Drizzle the honey vinaigrette over the carrots, turning to coat well. Sprinkle the pistachios on top. Return the carrots to the oven and roast until caramelized, about 5 minutes longer. Serve warm.

LEARN TOGETHER

Cooking together is as much about discovering
each other's cravings as it is about how to satisfy them.
Whether you dream of garlicky mashed potatoes on a cold
winter night or lemon-infused grilled asparagus at the
start of spring, sharing your culinary passions is a joyous
process. In these pages, you'll find updated classics
to satisfy both of you, along with plenty of delicious
new discoveries to try for the first time together.

Caramelized Brussels Sprouts with Bacon & Maple Vinaigrette

Roasting produces some of the tastiest, naturally sweet Brussels sprouts you'll ever eat. As you trim each head, snap off the outer leaves, toss them with olive oil and salt, and roast them separately for 10 minutes to make crisp chips—a delicious bonus.

SERVES 4

1½ lb (750 g) Brussels sprouts

2 Tbsp olive oil

Salt and freshly ground pepper

3 thick slices bacon, chopped

½ cup (2 oz/60 g) pecans, coarsely chopped

2 Tbsp maple syrup

2 Tbsp sherry vinegar

Preheat the oven to 425°F (220°C). Line a rimmed baking sheet with parchment paper.

Using a paring knife, trim off the base of each Brussels sprout, then cut lengthwise into quarters. Place the sprout quarters in a bowl, add the olive oil and a pinch of salt, and toss gently until evenly coated. Spread the sprouts in a single layer on the prepared baking sheet and roast until tender and spotted with brown, about 25 minutes.

While the sprouts are cooking, in a nonstick frying pan over medium heat, cook the bacon, stirring as needed to prevent burning, until almost crisp, about 7 minutes. Stir in the pecans and then the maple syrup and continue to sauté until the mixture is bubbly, about 2 minutes. Remove the pan from the heat and set aside.

When the Brussels sprouts are ready, transfer them to a serving bowl. Return the frying pan with the bacon mixture to medium-high heat. When the mixture starts to sizzle, stir in the vinegar and let cook until bubbly, about 10 seconds. Pour the bacon mixture over the sprouts, carefully scraping every bit from the pan. Season with pepper, toss well, and serve.

Roasted Endive Spears Wrapped in Prosciutto

Elegant, pale Belgian endives look particularly chic belted with prosciutto. They make a lovely side dish for roast chicken (page 170) or crab (page 155), or most other simple preparations. In the market, look for endives that are tightly furled and free of blemishes.

SERVES 4

4 heads Belgian endive, trimmed

8 paper-thin slices prosciutto

3 Tbsp olive oil, plus more as needed

½ cup (4 fl oz/125 ml) vegetable or chicken broth

1 Tbsp unsalted butter

¼ cup (1 oz/30 g) shredded Asiago or Parmesan cheese

Freshly ground pepper

Minced fresh flat-leaf parsley for garnish

Preheat the oven to 400°F (200°C). Halve the endives lengthwise. With a slice of prosciutto, wrap each endive half around the middle. If the prosciutto slice is too short, cut it in half lengthwise and wrap the pieces end to end.

Select a baking dish just large enough to accommodate the endive halves in a snug single layer and reserve.

In a large sauté pan over medium-high heat, warm the oil until it ripples. Working in batches and adding more oil as needed, place the endives, cut side down, in a single layer in the pan and cook until slightly browned on the cut sides, about 1½ minutes. Using tongs, turn the endives over and brown lightly on the second side, about 1 minute longer. Transfer the endives to the reserved baking dish.

Pour the broth into the sauté pan and scrape up any browned bits from the pan bottom. Swirl in the butter until it melts, then pour over and around the endives in the baking dish. Sprinkle the cheese evenly over the top. Roast until the endives are tender when pierced with a knife and the cheese is browned and crusty, 30–35 minutes.

Remove the endives from the oven, grind pepper over the top, and place on a warmed platter or individual plates. Spoon over the cooking juices, sprinkle with parsley, and serve hot.

Pan-Grilled Radicchio with Olive-Caper Salsa

Naturally bitter radicchio becomes sweeter when charred, creating the perfect flavor counterpoint to a briny green salsa. Ready the salsa up to a day in advance, and this Italian side dish will come together in minutes. Toasted walnuts add a final touch of flavor and crunch.

SERVES 4

2 teaspoons olive oil

⅓ cup (1½ oz/40 g) chopped walnuts

FOR THE OLIVE-CAPER SALSA

1 cup (1½ oz/45 g) firmly packed fresh flat-leaf parsley leaves

¼ cup (1¼ oz/35 g) pitted Kalamata olives

¼ cup (1¼ oz/35 g) small pitted green olives

1 Tbsp drained capers

1 Tbsp finely chopped shallot

½ cup (4 fl oz/125 ml) extra-virgin olive oil

4 heads Treviso or round radicchio, about 1½ lb (750 g) total weight

In a small frying pan over medium-low heat, warm the olive oil. Add the walnuts and toast, stirring occasionally, until pale golden, about 5 minutes. Set aside.

To make the olive-caper salsa, in a food processor, combine the parsley, both kinds of olives, capers, and shallot and pulse until finely chopped. Transfer to a bowl and stir in the olive oil, reserving 1 tablespoon.

Remove any discolored or wilted leaves from the radicchio. If using Treviso, cut in half lengthwise. If using round radicchio, cut into thick wedges. Place the pieces cut sides up and brush with the reserved oil.

Preheat a stove-top grill pan or griddle over medium-high heat. Place the radicchio, cut sides down, on the pan and cook, turning once, until wilted and slightly browned, about 2 minutes on each side.

Arrange the radicchio on a platter, spoon the salsa evenly over the top, and sprinkle with the walnuts. Serve warm.

italian classic

In Italy, radicchio is seldom seen in salads.
Italians prefer the tender chicory seared
(as here), grilled, or roasted—the best way
to savor its distinctive flavor.

spice it up

Cumin, paprika, and coriander are common in North African cuisine.
Add fresh mint and cilantro to the basil for more herb-infused flavor.

Braised Moroccan Eggplant

In the past, cooks salted cut raw eggplant to temper the bitterness, but that quality has been bred out. Nowadays, salting is a good way to reduce the amount of oil this versatile vegetable absorbs. Look for small, oblong eggplants in farmers' markets or specialty grocery stores.

SERVES 4

4 Japanese eggplants, about 1 lb (500 g), or other small, oblong eggplants

Salt

1 can (14 oz/440 g) whole plum tomatoes with juices

¼ cup (2 fl oz/60 ml) olive oil

2 cloves garlic, smashed

1 tsp ground cumin

1 tsp paprika

½ tsp ground coriander

Fresh basil leaves for garnish

2 Tbsp minced preserved lemon peel (optional)

Trim the eggplants and cut into halves or slices. Put the eggplant into a colander, sprinkle with 1 teaspoon salt, and toss to coat evenly. Set the colander in a sink and let the eggplant stand for 10 minutes (liquid will bead up on the flesh). Meanwhile, pour the tomatoes and their juices into a bowl and crush the tomatoes with your hand or a potato masher. Set aside.

In a large sauté pan or wok over medium-high heat, warm the oil and garlic, swirling the pan to flavor the oil, until the garlic starts to sizzle but does not color, about 1 minute. Add the salted eggplant and stir until well coated. Pour in ¼ cup (2 fl oz/60 ml) water and bring to a boil. Cover, reduce heat to medium-low, and cook until the eggplant is tender, about 10 minutes. Uncover and gently stir in the tomatoes, cumin, paprika, and coriander. Raise the heat to medium-high and let cook at a brisk simmer, shaking the pan occasionally, until the tomatoes thicken, about 10 minutes longer.

Remove from the heat and discard the garlic, if desired. Transfer the eggplant to a serving dish, sprinkle with the basil leaves and the preserved lemon, if using. Serve warm or at room temperature.

CHAPTER SEVEN

DESSERTS

I love you more than dessert

Crème Brûlée with Caramelized Blood Oranges

In this elegant dessert, a thick layer of vanilla custard is topped with a brittle sugar crust and caramel-coated slices of blood orange. You can caramelize sugar under the broiler, but a kitchen torch works better.

MAKES 3–4 CRÈMES BRÛLÉES

1½ cups (12 fl oz/375 ml) heavy cream

¼ cup (2 oz/60 g) granulated sugar

Pinch of salt

½ vanilla bean

4 large egg yolks

FOR THE CARAMELIZED BLOOD ORANGE

1 blood orange, ends trimmed, peel cut off, fruit sliced, and any seeds removed

2 Tbsp (1 oz/30 g) granulated sugar

3–4 tsp superfine sugar

caramelizing sugar

Prepare a kitchen torch or preheat a broiler. To use a torch, direct the flame over one section of sugar at a time, moving on only when each section becomes caramelized, until all are evenly browned. To use the broiler, preheat until very hot. Place the sugar-topped custards on a baking sheet and slide under the broiler about 3 inches (7.5 cm) from the heat source. (Watch carefully to prevent burning.)

Preheat the oven to 300°F (150°C). Have ready 3–4 ramekins, each ½–1 cup (4–8 fl oz/125–250 ml), and a baking pan large enough to hold the cups in a single layer.

In a saucepan, stir together the cream, granulated sugar, and salt. Using the tip of a sharp knife, split the vanilla bean and scrape the seeds into the cream. Add the pod and bring to a very gentle boil over medium heat, stirring constantly. Turn off the heat, cover, and let stand for 20 minutes.

Place the egg yolks in a bowl. Gradually whisk in the warm cream mixture. Pour through a fine-mesh sieve into a measuring pitcher. Divide the mixture evenly among the custard cups. Place the cups in the baking pan. Pour hot water into the pan to reach halfway up the sides of the cups. Bake until the custards are firm at the edges but still tremble in the center when shaken gently, 30–35 minutes.

Remove the pan from the oven, transfer the cups to a wire rack, and let cool. Cover with plastic wrap pressed directly onto the surface of the custards and refrigerate until thoroughly chilled, at least 2 hours or up to 2 days.

To make the caramelized orange, in a saucepan over medium-high heat, stir together the granulated sugar and 1 tablespoon water. Cook, swirling the pan occasionally, until the syrup turns a deep amber caramel. Remove from the heat, add the orange slices, and swirl the pan to coat them.

Just before serving, sprinkle each custard with a thin, even layer of about 1 teaspoon superfine sugar and caramelize (see note at left). Set the custards aside to harden for a few minutes, then top with some of the caramelized orange slices.

choose fruit in season

If blood oranges or similar citrus are not
in season, try blackberries, figs, or sliced
pear depending upon the time of year.

Salted Caramel Apple Pie

Granny Smith apples are called for here, but any sweet-tart apple that holds its shape in the oven, such as Cameo, Braeburn, or Cripps Pink, would also work. Store any leftover pie at room temperature for up to 2 days or in the refrigerator for up to 5 days.

SERVES 8–10

Double-Crust Flaky Pie Dough (page 250)

1½ cups (12 oz/375 g) granulated sugar

1 Tbsp plus 1 tsp fresh lemon juice

1½ cups (375 ml) heavy cream

2 tsp salt

5 lb (2.5 kg) Granny Smith apples, peeled, cored, and each apple cut into 8 slices

½ cup (3½ oz/105 g) firmly packed light brown sugar

½ tsp ground cinnamon

¼ tsp ground nutmeg

3 Tbsp cornstarch

1 large egg beaten with 1 tsp water

Turbinado sugar for sprinkling

Flaky sea salt such as Maldon for sprinkling

Make the pie dough. Roll out half of the dough into a 12-inch (30-cm) round; keep the remaining half refrigerated. Fit the round into a 9-inch (23-cm) deep-dish pie dish and trim the edge flush with the rim. Refrigerate for 30 minutes.

In a large saucepan over medium heat, combine the granulated sugar, ¼ cup (60 ml) water, and the 1 teaspoon lemon juice. Cook until the mixture bubbles vigorously and turns a golden amber color, about 9 minutes. Remove from the heat and carefully add the cream, stirring until blended. Stir in 1½ teaspoons of the salt and let cool until just warm.

In a large pot over medium heat, stir together the apples, brown sugar, cinnamon, nutmeg, and the 1 tablespoon lemon juice. Cover and cook, stirring occasionally, until the apples are just tender, 10–12 minutes. Uncover and let cool. Stir in the cornstarch, the remaining ½ teaspoon salt, and ¾ cup (180 ml) of the caramel sauce. Cover the remaining sauce and refrigerate until ready to serve.

Meanwhile, preheat the oven to 350°F (180°C). Roll out the remaining dough into a 12-inch (30-cm) round. Pour the filling into the dough-lined pie dish. Place the flat dough round over the filling, trim the edge flush with the rim, and crimp to seal and form a decorative edge. Brush the crust with the egg mixture and sprinkle with turbinado sugar. Place the pie dish on a baking sheet.

Bake until the crust is golden brown and the filling is bubbling, about 1 hour, covering the top and edges loosely with aluminum foil if they brown too quickly. Let cool on a wire rack for at least 4 hours, or preferably overnight, before serving.

To serve, reheat the reserved caramel sauce over low heat until just warm. Sprinkle the pie with flaky sea salt, slice, and serve with the sauce.

Individual Peach Crisps

Simple fruit crisps like these are one of the easiest desserts to prepare, and can be among the most delicious. You can trade the peaches for nectarines, and the cinnamon for nutmeg or coriander. Finish off each serving with a scoop of vanilla ice cream.

MAKES 4–6 INDIVIDUAL PEACH CRISPS

FOR THE TOPPING

Scant 1⅓ cups (7 oz/220 g) all-purpose flour

⅓ cup (2½ oz/75 g) firmly packed brown sugar

⅓ cup (3 oz/90 g) granulated sugar

¼ tsp salt

¼ tsp ground cinnamon

1 cup (5½ oz/170 g) toasted whole raw almonds, coarsely chopped

¾ cup (6 oz/185 g) cold unsalted butter, plus more for greasing

FOR THE FRUIT

6 ripe peaches

Pinch of salt

2 Tbsp granulated sugar

To make the topping, whisk together the flour, both sugars, the salt, and the cinnamon. Stir in the almonds. Cut the butter into small pieces and work into the flour mixture with your fingertips, rubbing and smearing, until the topping comes together and has a crumbly texture.

Preheat the oven to 350°F (180°C). Grease 4–6 individual gratin dishes with butter.

To prepare the fruit, bring a large pot of water to a boil and ready a large bowl of ice water. Using a slotted spoon, immerse the peaches in the boiling water for about 30 seconds, depending on the ripeness, then transfer to the bowl of ice water. Slip off and discard the skins. Halve each peach and discard the pits. Slice each half into wedges and place in a bowl. Add the salt and granulated sugar. Toss to mix. Spoon the fruit into the prepared gratin dishes.

Sprinkle the topping evenly over the fruit. (Store any remaining topping in a covered container in the refrigerator for up to 5 days, or freeze for up to 1 month.) Place the gratin dishes on a baking sheet to catch any drips and place the baking sheet in the oven. Bake until the topping is golden brown and the fruit juices have begun to bubble, 20–25 minutes. Remove from the oven and let cool slightly before serving.

finish with flourish
Even when it's just the two of you,
a fresh garnish—like the golden
currants and fresh elderflowers
used here—makes any dessert all
the more special.

Strawberry-Rhubarb Galette

The sweetness of strawberries mellows the slight bitterness of rhubarb in this rustic dessert. Loosely combined within the delicate confines of a sweet buttery crust, the two star ingredients of late spring are at their very best. A food processor makes pastry preparation a breeze.

MAKES ONE 9-INCH (23-CM) GALETTE

FOR THE CRUST

2 cups (10 oz/315 g) all-purpose flour, plus more for dusting

½ tsp sugar

¼ tsp salt

¾ cup (6 oz/185 g) cold unsalted butter, cut into pieces

⅓ cup (3 fl oz/80 ml) ice water

1½ lb (24 oz/750 g) strawberries, hulled and halved

1 thin stalk rhubarb (about 5 oz/155 g), trimmed and cut into 2-inch (5-cm) pieces

½ cup (4 oz/125 g) sugar

¼ cup (1½ oz/45 g) all-purpose flour

1 Tbsp fresh lemon juice or 1 Tbsp fresh orange juice mixed with the finely grated zest of 1 orange

Fresh currants for garnish (optional)

Elderflowers for garnish (optional)

To make the crust, in a food processor, combine the flour, sugar, and salt and pulse to mix. Scatter the butter around the bowl and pulse just until the mixture resembles coarse crumbs. With the motor running, drizzle in the ice water and process just until a ball of dough begins to form. Turn the dough out onto a lightly floured work surface and press it into a disk. Wrap tightly in plastic wrap and refrigerate for at least 1 hour and up to overnight. Remove the dough from the refrigerator about 20 minutes before you plan to roll it out.

Meanwhile, in a large bowl, combine the strawberries, rhubarb, sugar, flour, and lemon juice or orange juice and zest. Set aside, stirring occasionally, until the sugar has dissolved and the mixture coats the fruit.

Preheat the oven to 425°F (220°C). Line a baking sheet with parchment paper. Place the dough on a lightly floured work surface and roll out into a 13-inch (33-cm) round. Fold the round in half, transfer to the prepared sheet, and unfold.

Scrape the filling and accumulated juices onto the center of the dough, leaving a 2-inch (5-cm) border uncovered around the edge. Fold the edge up and over onto the filling, forming loose pleats. Bake until the filling is bubbling, the rhubarb is tender when pierced with a sharp knife, and the pastry is golden brown, 25–35 minutes.

Transfer the galette to a wire rack and let cool. Garnish with fresh currants and elderflowers, if desired. Cut into wedges and serve.

Fresh Lemon Mousse

Lemon, cream, and egg yolks strike the right balance of rich and flavorful in this sunny yellow pudding. It goes together quickly, is delicious as is or topped with berries or chopped fresh mint, and will keep for up to a day—if it isn't eaten for a midnight snack.

SERVES 3–4

1 tsp unflavored gelatin

½ cup (4 oz/125 g) granulated sugar

Pinch of salt

1 tsp finely grated lemon zest

⅓ cup (2½ fl oz/80 ml) fresh lemon juice (from about 8 lemons)

2 egg yolks

1 cup (8 fl oz/250 ml) heavy cream

2 Tbsp confectioners' sugar

Pour 2 tablespoons water into a saucepan and sprinkle with the gelatin. Let stand until the gelatin softens and swells, 5–10 minutes. Stir in the granulated sugar, salt, lemon zest and juice, and egg yolks. Cook over medium heat, stirring constantly, until the mixture thickens and the gelatin melts completely, 5–6 minutes. Do not boil.

Have ready a bowl of ice. Set the saucepan in the bowl of ice and stir until the mixture is cool to the touch. Remove the pan from the ice and set aside.

In a bowl, using an electric mixer, beat the cream and confectioners' sugar on medium speed until soft peaks form, 4–6 minutes. Using a spatula, fold in the lemon mixture until smooth.

Spoon the mousse into 3–4 custard cups. Refrigerate the mousse until chilled, 2–3 hours. Remove from the refrigerator about 20 minutes before serving.

Spice-Roasted Banana Sundae

Roasting bananas enhances their sweetness, and the juices they release mix with a splash of cream and a bit of sugar to create a thick pan sauce. The number of sundaes you make is easy to vary using this simple recipe. Refrigerate any leftover chocolate sauce for up to a week.

SERVES 6

6 large firm-ripe bananas, peeled

¼ tsp ground cinnamon

¼ tsp ground nutmeg

1–2 Tbsp sugar

2 Tbsp heavy cream

FOR THE CHOCOLATE SAUCE

12 oz (375 g) semisweet chocolate, chopped

2 oz (60 g) unsweetened chocolate, chopped

1½ cups (12 fl oz/375 ml) heavy cream

1 Tbsp vanilla extract, plus more as needed

1½ qt (1.5 l) vanilla or cinnamon ice cream

Preheat the oven to 375°F (190°C).

Arrange the bananas in a single layer in a small baking pan. Lightly dust them with the cinnamon, nutmeg, and sugar. Drizzle with the heavy cream. Roast until the bananas have softened but still hold their shape and the reduced cream forms a bubbly sauce, about 30 minutes.

Meanwhile, make the chocolate sauce: In a large heatproof bowl set over (but not touching) simmering water in a saucepan, melt the chocolates together. Pour in the cream in a steady stream, whisking constantly until smooth. Stir in the vanilla. Taste and adjust the flavoring. Keep warm.

When the bananas are ready, place one on each of 6 warmed plates and drizzle the banana pan juices over the top. Top each with a scoop of ice cream and drizzle with some warm chocolate sauce. Serve warm, passing the remaining chocolate sauce at the table.

Fresh Strawberry Ice Cream

This recipe combines the richness of a custard-based ice cream with the vibrancy of fresh strawberries. Crush the berries to create juicy bits of flavor in each bite, or keep them in larger pieces for chunky appeal.

MAKES ABOUT 1½ QUARTS (1.5 L)

3 cups (12 oz/375 g) fresh strawberries, hulled and halved

⅔ cup (5 oz/155 g) plus 2 Tbsp sugar

2 tsp fresh lemon juice

1 cup (8 fl oz/250 ml) heavy cream

1 cup (8 fl oz/250 ml) half-and-half

3 large egg yolks

Pinch of salt

In a bowl, combine the berries, the 2 tablespoons sugar, and the lemon juice and lightly crush with a fork. Cover and let stand for about 1 hour.

In a heavy saucepan, combine the cream and half-and-half. Warm over medium-high heat, stirring occasionally, just until the mixture barely comes to a simmer, about 5 minutes. Remove from the heat.

Meanwhile, in a heatproof bowl, combine the egg yolks, the ⅔ cup (5 oz/155 g) sugar, and the salt. Whisk vigorously until the mixture lightens in color and doubles in volume, about 2 minutes. Slowly whisk about 1 cup (8 fl oz/250 ml) of the warm cream mixture into the egg mixture, whisking until smooth. Pour the egg-cream mixture back into the saucepan, whisking constantly, and place over medium heat. Using a wooden spoon, stir until the mixture thickens enough to coat the back of the spoon, 1–2 minutes. Do not boil.

Meanwhile, prepare a large bowl of ice and nest a smaller heatproof bowl inside. Pour the custard through a fine-mesh sieve into the smaller bowl and stir occasionally until cool. Remove the bowl from the ice, stir in the strawberry mixture, cover with plastic wrap, and refrigerate until very cold, at least 4 hours or up to 1 day.

Pour the cold custard into an ice-cream maker and freeze according to the manufacturer's instructions. Spoon the ice cream into a freezer-safe container and place parchment paper or waxed paper directly over the top. Cover tightly and freeze until firm, at least 2 hours or up to 3 days.

fresh strawberry

an anytime dessert

There's nothing like sharing a late-night carton of ice cream and a good movie. Of course, ice creams like these make nifty desserts at any time of the day or night.

coffee crunch

Coffee Crunch
Ice Cream

*Freshly ground dark-roasted coffee beans, such as French or Italian
roast, give this candy-studded ice cream the most intense flavor.
For the crunch, feel free to substitute chopped nuts, crumbled
Heath bars, or other candy in place of the coffee-flavored variety.*

MAKE ABOUT 1 QUART (32 FL OZ/1 L)

1½ cups (12 fl oz/375 ml) whole milk

1½ cups (12 fl oz/375 ml) heavy cream

1 cup (8 fl oz/250 ml) strongly brewed
dark-roast coffee, chilled

½ cup plus 1 Tbsp sugar

Pinch of salt

1 tsp vanilla extract

½ cup (2 oz/60 g) coffee-flavored
hard candies

In a small bowl, combine the milk, cream, and brewed
coffee.

In a large bowl, combine the sugar and salt. Add the
milk mixture and whisk until the sugar dissolves. Add the
vanilla and stir to combine. Set aside, stirring occasionally,
to allow the flavors to blend, about 15 minutes. Cover
and refrigerate the mixture until chilled, at least 3 hours
or up to 8 hours.

Pour the mixture into an ice-cream maker and churn
according to the manufacturer's instructions.

Meanwhile, place the candies in a resealable plastic bag
and, using a meat pounder or rolling pin, crush them
into small bits. Add the candy during the last minute
of churning. Transfer the ice cream to a freezer-safe
container. Cover and freeze until firm, at least 3 hours
or up to 3 days.

Individual Tiramisus with Espresso & Rum

Delicate ladyfingers soaked in espresso and rum, layered with mascarpone custard, and dusted with cocoa make up this favorite Italian dessert. Serve it in large goblets or small glass bowls. Cut the ladyfingers to fit your vessel of choice, using only as many as needed.

SERVES 4

¼ cup (2 oz/60 g) sugar

¾ cup (12 fl oz/375 ml) freshly brewed espresso

3 Tbsp dark rum

FOR THE FILLING

3 Tbsp sugar

3 large egg yolks

¼ cup (2 fl oz/60 ml) heavy cream

¾ cup (6 oz/180 g) mascarpone cheese

¾ tsp vanilla extract

24 ladyfingers or 12 thin slices of store-bought pound cake

Unsweetened cocoa powder for dusting

In a small saucepan over medium heat, bring the sugar and 2 tablespoons water to a simmer and cook, stirring, until the sugar is dissolved, about 3 minutes. Remove from the heat, stir in the espresso, and let cool. Stir in the rum. Pour the mixture into a wide, shallow bowl and set aside.

To make the filling, fill a saucepan with about 2 inches (5 cm) of water and bring to a bare simmer over medium-low heat. In a heatproof bowl, whisk together the sugar and egg yolks until the sugar has dissolved and the mixture is pale yellow and creamy, about 2 minutes. Place the bowl over (but not touching) the water. Using an electric mixer, beat the yolk mixture on medium speed until thick and tripled in volume, about 6 minutes. Remove the bowl from the heat and let cool, stirring often.

In another bowl, beat the cream on medium-high speed until stiff peaks form.

Add the mascarpone and vanilla to the cooled yolk mixture. Beat with the mixer on medium speed just until smooth and well blended. Using a large spatula, fold the whipped cream into the yolk mixture just until combined.

Place two ladyfingers or one slice of pound cake (cut to fit) in the bottom of each of 4 individual glass dessert bowls or goblets. Brush liberally with the espresso mixture. Using the spatula, evenly spread one-third of the filling over the ladyfingers. Place another layer of cake on top, brush with the espresso mixture, and spread evenly with half of the remaining filling. Place a third layer of the cake on top, brush with the remaining espresso mixture, then top evenly with the remaining filling. Gently tap each dish against the counter to settle the ingredients.

Cover with plastic wrap and refrigerate for at least 6 hours or up to overnight. Dust the tops with cocoa powder just before serving.

Sticky Lemon Bundt Cake

The sweet lemony flavor and wonderful versatility of this cake will make this a recipe you turn to again and again. The cake is delicious served on its own, but is particularly good when topped with dollops of lightly whipped cream and seasonal berries.

SERVES 6

1½ cups (12 oz/375 g) unsalted butter, at room temperature, plus more for greasing

3 cups (15 oz/425 g) all-purpose flour, preferably low-gluten, plus more for dusting

2 tsp baking powder

1 tsp salt

8 oz (250 g) cream cheese, at room temperature

2 cups (16 oz/500 g) sugar

6 large eggs

2 tsp vanilla extract

1 Tbsp finely grated lemon zest

¼ cup (2 fl oz/60 ml) fresh lemon juice

FOR THE LEMON SYRUP

1 Tbsp finely grated lemon zest

½ cup (4 fl oz/125 ml) fresh lemon juice

½ cup (4 oz/125 g) sugar

Lemon slices or strips of lemon zest for garnish (optional)

Preheat the oven to 350°F (180°C). Lightly butter a 10-cup (2.5-l) bundt pan. Dust with flour and tap out the excess.

In a large bowl, sift together the flour, baking powder, and salt. Set aside.

In an electric mixer fitted with the paddle attachment, cream together the butter and cream cheese on medium-high speed until smooth, about 3 minutes. Reduce the speed to medium and add the sugar. Continue to beat until fluffy, about 2 minutes longer. Beat in the eggs one at a time, beating well after each addition. Remove the bowl and, using a spatula, fold in the flour mixture until incorporated. Stir in the vanilla and lemon zest and juice.

Pour the batter into the prepared bundt pan and smooth the top with the spatula. Bake until a toothpick inserted into the center comes out clean, about 1 hour. Transfer to a wire rack and let cool in the pan for 30 minutes.

While the cake is baking, make the lemon syrup. In a nonreactive saucepan over medium heat, combine the lemon zest, lemon juice, and sugar, stirring until the sugar is dissolved. Bring to a boil, then reduce the heat to low. Simmer until reduced by one-third, 10–15 minutes. Remove from the heat and set aside until ready to use.

To loosen the cake, tap the side of the pan gently on a work surface. Invert a flat cake plate or pedestal over the pan and invert the plate and the pan together. Tap the bottom of the pan and lift it off. While the cake is still warm, poke holes in the surface with a toothpick, then brush all over with lemon syrup, allowing the cake to absorb the syrup before applying more. Let cool for 30 minutes longer.

Just before serving, slice the cake and garnish with lemon slices, if you like.

MODERN
HEIRLOOM

TREAT YOURSELVES

MAKE EVERY MOMENT A SWEET ONE

Whether it is a fresh-from-the-oven apple pie
or a lemon bundt cake dressed up with a sticky glaze,
dessert is a welcome indulgence that becomes even
more special when it's homemade. Take the time to bake
cookies together on a lazy Sunday afternoon or to whip up
chocolate-dipped strawberries for an at-home date night.
When you're sweet on each other, it is always good
to bring a little sugar into the kitchen.

Plum Upside-Down Cake

Upside-down cakes emerge from the oven looking quite plain, until they are unmolded to reveal their beautiful caramelized fruit. To make sure that step goes smoothly, run a knife around the inside edge of the pan before inverting it and then let the cake release naturally.

SERVES 8

3 Tbsp unsalted butter plus ½ cup (4 oz/125 g), at room temperature

¾ cup (6 oz/185 g) firmly packed light brown sugar

5 or 6 ripe but firm plums such as Santa Rosa, about ½ lb (750 g) total weight, halved, pitted, and quartered

1⅓ cups (5½ oz/170 g) cake flour

1½ tsp baking powder

¼ tsp salt

¾ cup (6 oz/185 g) granulated sugar

2 large eggs

1 tsp vanilla extract

⅔ cup (5 fl oz/160 ml) buttermilk

Vanilla ice cream for serving

In a 10-inch (25-cm) cast-iron frying pan over medium heat, melt the 3 tablespoons butter. Add the brown sugar and cook, stirring, until the sugar melts and bubbles, about 4 minutes. Let cool slightly. Carefully arrange the plum quarters in the pan in concentric circles.

Preheat the oven to 375°F (190°C). In a bowl, sift together the flour, baking powder, and salt. In the bowl of an electric mixer fitted with the paddle attachment, beat the ½ cup (4 oz/125 g) butter and the granulated sugar on medium-high speed until light and fluffy, 2–3 minutes. Add the eggs one at a time, beating well after each addition. Beat in the vanilla. On low speed, stir in half of the flour mixture, then the buttermilk and the remaining flour mixture, beating just until combined.

Dollop the batter over the fruit and smooth as evenly as you can. Bake until a toothpick inserted into the center of the cake comes out clean, about 40 minutes. Let cool in the pan on a wire rack for about 15 minutes.

Place a serving plate, upside down, over the pan. Wearing oven mitts, carefully invert the plate and pan. Cut the cake into wedges and serve with big scoops of vanilla ice cream.

Naked Gluten-Free Almond Cake

When cake is as good as this one, it's best if the frosting is kept to a bare (quite literally!) minimum. Cover the cake with just a thin sweep of frosting, leaving the layers exposed, then finish with a mound of fresh berries or a heap of edible blossoms on top.

SERVES 8

Butter for greasing

2¼ cups (7 oz/200 g) almond meal

¾ tsp baking soda

½ tsp ground cinnamon

6 large eggs, separated

⅔ cup (5 oz/155 g) sugar

2 Tbsp grated lemon zest

2 Tbsp fresh lemon juice

½ tsp salt

¼ tsp cream of tartar

FOR THE VANILLA FROSTING

2¼ cups (9 oz/280 g) confectioners' sugar

½ cup (4 oz/125 g) cream cheese, at room temperature

¾ cup (6 oz/185 g) unsalted butter, at room temperature

1 Tbsp milk

1 tsp vanilla extract

2 cups (8 oz/250 g) mixed fresh berries, or 1 cup (1 oz/30 g) fresh edible blossoms

Preheat the oven to 350°F (180°C). Butter two 8-inch (20-cm) round cake pans. Line the bottoms with parchment paper cut to fit exactly and butter the parchment.

In a bowl, combine the almond meal, baking soda, and cinnamon. In a large bowl, whisk together the egg yolks, ⅓ cup (2½ oz/80 g) of the sugar and the lemon zest and juice until smooth.

In an electric stand mixer, beat the egg whites on medium speed until frothy, about 2 minutes. Add the salt and cream of tartar and beat on medium-high speed until soft peaks form, about 2 minutes. Gradually add the remaining ⅓ cup (2½ oz/80 g) sugar, beating until stiff peaks form.

Add the almond mixture to the egg yolk mixture, stirring with a spatula. Fold in one-third of the beaten egg whites to lighten the batter. Then, in 2 additions, gently fold in the remaining whites just until incorporated. Spoon the batter into the prepared pans, dividing it evenly.

Bake the cakes until a toothpick inserted into a center comes out clean, about 25 minutes. Transfer the cakes to wire racks. Using a small, sharp knife, cut around the cakes' edges to loosen. Let cool completely in the pans.

To make the frosting, in the bowl of an electric mixer, combine the sugar, cream cheese, butter, milk and vanilla. Beat on medium speed until light and fluffy, 3–4 minutes.

To assemble the cake, remove the cakes from the pans. Put one cake, rounded side up, on a plate. Spread an even layer of frosting over the top. Invert the second cake over the frosting. Spread the remaining frosting over the cake, filling in the gap between the layers first, then smoothing a thin coat of frosting on the top and a sheer coat on the sides. Top with berries or blossoms. Cut into wedges to serve.

Chocolate-Hazelnut Torte

Known in French as Reine de Saba, *this rich cake was made popular in the United States by Julia Child. Vary the flavor by substituting walnuts or pecans for the almonds, or adding a few drops of liqueur or extract to the ganache. This dense and chocolatey cake is entirely gluten-free, though no one will know unless you tell them.*

MAKES ONE 10-INCH (25-CM) CAKE

¾ cup (6 oz/185 g) unsalted butter, at room temperature, plus more for greasing

All-purpose flour for dusting

8 oz (250 g) bittersweet chocolate, chopped

¾ cup (6 oz/185 g) sugar

6 extra-large eggs, separated, at room temperature

1½ cups (6 oz/185 g) ground skinned hazelnuts, ground blanched almonds, or ground pecans

FOR THE GANACHE

1 cup (8 fl oz/250 ml) heavy cream

10 oz (315 g) semisweet or bittersweet chocolate, chopped

Position a rack in the lower third of the oven and preheat to 350°F (180°C). Butter the bottom and sides of a 10-inch (25-cm) round springform pan with 3-inch (7.5-cm) sides and line the bottom with parchment paper. Butter the paper and dust with flour.

In a heatproof bowl set over (but not touching) simmering water in a saucepan, heat the chocolate, stirring, until melted and smooth. Remove from the heat and let cool slightly.

In a bowl, using an electric mixer on high speed, beat the butter with the sugar until light and fluffy, 8–10 minutes. Add the egg yolks, one at a time, beating well after each addition. Beat in the chocolate and the nuts.

In a large bowl, using clean beaters, beat the egg whites on medium-high speed until stiff and glossy but not dry. Using a spatula, gently but thoroughly fold the egg whites into the chocolate mixture. Pour into the prepared pan and smooth the top with the spatula.

Bake the cake until the top puffs, about 50 minutes; do not overbake. Let cool in the pan on a wire rack for 15 minutes. Remove the pan sides. Invert the cake onto the rack and let cool completely, then peel off the parchment.

While the cake is cooling, make the ganache. In a small saucepan over medium heat, gently warm the cream until small bubbles appear around the edge of the pan. Remove from the heat. Add the chocolate and stir gently until melted and smooth.

Invert the cake onto a serving plate and, using an icing spatula, spread the warm ganache over the top and sides. Let stand until the ganache sets before serving.

a sprinkle of gold dust
Food-grade luster dust is sold online and in specialty baking shops. It adds an elegant last-minute flourish to glazed cakes and other desserts.

Old-Fashioned Angel Food Cake

The best angel food cake is light, airy, and just slightly sweet. For a perfect result, have your bowl and tools spotlessly clean and fold in the flour gently but fully. To maintain the cake's signature loft while serving, cut it with a serrated knife using a gentle sawing motion.

SERVES 8–10

½ cup (2 oz/60 g) confectioners' sugar

1 cup (4 oz/125 g) cake flour

2 cups (16 fl oz/500 ml) egg whites (from about 14 large eggs), at room temperature

2 tsp cream of tartar

½ tsp salt

1½ cups (12 oz/375 g) granulated sugar

1 tsp vanilla extract

½ tsp almond extract

seasonal variations

Fluffy, vanilla-scented angel food cake is an ideal base for fresh fruits in season. Try sweetened sliced strawberries or cherries in spring, and stone fruit in summer. In colder months, toast wedges of the cake under the broiler until warm and crisp on the outside before topping them with spiced and sautéed apple or pear slices in autumn, and sweet, ginger-infused citrus in winter.

Position a rack in the lower third of the oven, making sure there is plenty of headroom for the cake, and preheat the oven to 350°F (180°C). Have ready an ungreased 10-inch (25-cm) angel food cake pan.

In a small bowl, sift together the confectioners' sugar and flour. In a bowl, using an electric mixer on medium speed, beat the egg whites, cream of tartar, and salt until foamy. Increase the speed to high, then slowly pour in the granulated sugar, beating just until soft peaks form. Add the vanilla and almond extracts and beat for 30 seconds longer, just until stiff, glossy peaks form. Do not overbeat.

Using a spatula, scrape the beaten egg whites into a large bowl. Gently and quickly fold the flour mixture into the egg whites in 3 equal batches, making sure no pockets of flour remain. Scoop the batter into the cake pan and smooth the top. Tap the pan lightly against the counter to remove any large air pockets.

Bake until golden and puffed and a thin skewer inserted near the center comes out clean, 40–45 minutes. Remove from the oven, let cool for 5 minutes, and then invert the pan over the neck of a wine bottle and let cool completely. To unmold, run a long, thin knife blade around the inside of the pan and the tube to loosen the cake. Invert the pan and tap gently until the cake slides out.

Spiced Gingerbread with Frosting

Especially during the holidays, a boldly spiced cake like this one could become a new family tradition. For added sparkle, sprinkle the frosted cake with tiny shards of crystallized ginger. Serve a pot of strong coffee or flutes of Champagne to balance its spicy sweetness.

SERVES 8–10

½ cup (4 oz/125 g) unsalted butter, melted, plus more for greasing

2 cups (10 oz/315 g) all-purpose flour

1 Tbsp ground ginger

1½ tsp ground cinnamon

½ tsp ground cloves

½ tsp finely ground black pepper

⅛ tsp cayenne pepper

¾ tsp salt

½ tsp baking powder

½ tsp baking soda

2 large eggs

1 cup (7 oz/220 g) firmly packed light brown sugar

⅔ cup (7½ oz/235 g) dark molasses

1 cup (8 fl oz/250 ml) whole milk

4-inch (10-cm) piece fresh ginger, peeled and grated

FOR THE FROSTING

½ lb (250 g) cream cheese, at room temperature

4 Tbsp (2 oz/60 g) unsalted butter, at room temperature

Pinch of salt

⅔ cup (2½ oz/75 g) confectioners' sugar, sifted

1 tsp dry sherry

Preheat the oven to 350°F (180°C). Butter an 8-inch (20-cm) square baking dish.

In a bowl, whisk together the flour, ground ginger, cinnamon, cloves, black pepper, cayenne, salt, baking powder, and baking soda.

In another bowl, whisk the eggs until blended, then add the brown sugar and whisk vigorously to combine. Whisk in the molasses and milk. Add the fresh ginger and whisk well.

Pour the egg mixture into the flour mixture and stir with a spatula a few times to moisten the ingredients. While stirring, drizzle in the melted butter, mixing just until blended.

Scrape the batter into the prepared baking dish, spreading it evenly. Bake until the center springs back when pressed lightly with a fingertip and a toothpick inserted into the center comes out clean, about 40 minutes. Let cool in the pan on a wire rack.

While the cake is cooling, make the frosting. Using an electric mixer on medium-high speed, beat together the cream cheese, butter, and salt until light and creamy, 1–2 minutes. Add the confectioners' sugar and beat until smooth. Mix in the sherry.

Using an icing spatula, spread the frosting on the cooled cake. Cut the cake into squares and serve.

marshmallows

graham
crackers

flaked
coconut

chocolate
sauce

caramel
sauce

sea salt

cherries

strawberries

Brownies Five Ways

If the only brownies you have ever baked were from the recipe on the back of a brownie-mix box or a can of cocoa powder, you are in for a treat. Variations abound. Think beyond the brownie sundae and try a few of these.

basic brownies

¾ cup (6 oz/185 g) unsalted butter, plus more for greasing

1 cup (5 oz/155 g) all-purpose flour, plus more for dusting

½ tsp *each* baking soda and sea salt

6 oz (185 g) unsweetened chocolate, finely chopped

1 cup (8 oz/250 g) granulated sugar

1 cup (7 oz/220 g) firmly packed light brown sugar

4 large eggs, at room temperature

¼ cup (3 fl oz/80 g) light corn syrup, honey, or maple syrup

2 tsp vanilla extract

Preheat the oven to 350°F (180°C). Butter a 9-by-13-inch (23-by-33-cm) baking pan.

In a bowl, sift together the flour, baking soda, and salt. Set aside. In a saucepan over medium heat, melt the butter. Remove from the heat and add the unsweetened chocolate. Let stand for 3 minutes, then whisk until smooth. Whisk in both sugars until blended. Whisk in the eggs, one at a time, then whisk in the corn syrup and vanilla. Add the flour mixture and stir until combined. Spread the batter evenly in the prepared pan.

Bake until a toothpick inserted into the center comes out with a few moist crumbs attached, about 25 minutes. Let cool in the pan on a wire rack. Cut into squares.

MAKES ABOUT 12 BROWNIES

graham cracker
+
marshmallow

6 graham crackers

12 jumbo marshmallows

Prepare the brownie batter as directed. Just before spooning the batter into the pan, crush the graham crackers over the batter and stir until blended. Spread the batter evenly in the prepared pan. Top evenly with the marshmallows. Bake as directed.

caramel sauce
+
sea salt
+
macadamia nut

1 bag (14 oz/440 g) caramels

¼ cup (2 fl oz/60 ml) evaporated milk

2 Tbsp unsalted butter

1 tsp flaky sea salt

½ cup (2½ oz/ 75 g) chopped toasted macadamia nuts

Make the brownies as directed. In a small saucepan over medium heat, combine the caramels and milk. Heat, stirring often, until smooth, about 5 minutes. Stir in the butter. Top each square with a drizzle of caramel and a sprinkling of the salt and nuts.

sweet berry
+
hot fudge sauce

1 pint (12 oz/375 g) fresh strawberries or pitted cherries, halved

2 Tbsp sugar

1 cup (8 fl oz/250 ml) chocolate sauce

1 pint (16 oz/500 g) ice cream of choice

Make the brownies as directed. In a small bowl, mix the berries and sugar. Let stand until juicy, about 30 minutes. Warm the chocolate sauce in the microwave. Top each square with a scoop of ice cream, a spoonful of juicy berries, and a drizzle of the warm sauce.

coconut flake
+
chocolate chunk
+
pecan

3¾ cups (1½ lb/750 g) sweetened flaked coconut

1 package (11½ oz/330 g) semisweet chocolate chunks

1 can (14 oz fl/395 g) sweetened condensed milk

1 cup (5 oz/155 g) chopped pecans

Bake the brownie just until set, 16–18 minutes. Layer the coconut and chocolate over the brownie, then pour the condensed milk over the top. Sprinkle with the nuts. Finish baking.

Chocolate-Dipped Strawberries

The hardest part of this elegant dessert is finding the most beautiful strawberries and the best-quality chocolate. Make sure the berries are ripe and flavorful but neither bruised nor soft, and have them at room temperature and perfectly dry before dipping them.

MAKES 20-30 DIPPED STRAWBERRIES

1 cup (6 oz/185 g) good-quality semisweet chocolate chips

1 Tbsp vegetable shortening

1–2 pints (12–24 oz/375–750 g) large fresh strawberries

In a heatproof bowl set over (but not touching) simmering water in a saucepan, heat the chocolate chips and shortening, stirring occasionally with a spatula, until melted and smooth, 5–7 minutes. Remove the pan from the heat, but leave the bowl atop the pan to keep the chocolate warm.

Line a baking sheet with waxed paper. Holding each strawberry by its green hull or stem, dip it into the melted chocolate until it is about three-fourths covered. Use the spatula, if necessary, to help coat each strawberry with chocolate. Let the excess chocolate drip back into the bowl, then place each strawberry on the prepared baking sheet.

When all of the berries have been dipped, place the baking sheet in the refrigerator until the chocolate sets, 10–15 minutes. Transfer the chocolate-dipped berries to a serving plate. They are best eaten within a day. If necessary, cover loosely with waxed paper and store overnight in the refrigerator. Serve at room temperature.

live in the moment

These tantalizing chocolate-dipped bites are best on the day they're made, so make only as many as you can eat at one sitting.

sweet versatility

A crisp, yet chewy, buttery and nutty peanut butter cookie is a thing of beauty. But, if you're the type who likes to tamper with perfection, this iconic confection is deliciously adaptable. Pair it with caramel ice cream in a thick sandwich, stir shredded coconut and chopped crystallized ginger into the batter, or press caramels or small round chocolates into the cookie tops before baking.

Peanut Butter & Sea Salt Cookies

To dress up these cookies, use the tines of a fork to drizzle a little melted semisweet or bittersweet chocolate over each one after they cool. If you have the time, refrigerate the dough before shaping it, and the cookies will spread less in the oven.

MAKES ABOUT 2 DOZEN COOKIES

½ cup (4 oz/125 g) unsalted butter, at room temperature

¾ cup (5 oz/185 g) firmly packed light brown sugar

¼ cup (2 oz/60 g) granulated sugar

¾ cup (7½ oz/235 g) creamy peanut butter

1 large egg

½ tsp vanilla extract

1¼ cups (6½ oz/200 g) all-purpose flour

⅓ cup (2 oz/60 g) finely chopped unsalted raw peanuts

1 tsp baking soda

¼ tsp salt

About 1 Tbsp flaky sea salt such as Maldon

Preheat the oven to 350°F (180°C). Line 2 baking sheets with parchment paper.

In a large bowl, using an electric mixer on medium speed, beat the butter, both sugars, and peanut butter until blended. Add the egg and vanilla and beat until blended. Add the flour, peanuts, baking soda, and salt and beat on low speed until blended.

Shape the dough into 1½-inch (4-cm) balls, placing 12 balls at least 2 inches (5 cm) apart on each baking sheet. Dip a fork in flour, then press twice into each cookie to make a crisscross pattern, then sprinkle with flaky sea salt. Bake the cookies until golden, 8–10 minutes. Let the cookies cool on the pans for 5 minutes, then transfer to wire racks and let cool completely.

The Best Chocolate Chip Cookies

Big, chewy, buttery, with the perfect amount of chips and nuts—that's what makes these cookies the best. For the tastiest result, buy the finest chocolate your budget can handle.

MAKES ABOUT 3 DOZEN COOKIES

1 cup (4 oz/125 g) walnut pieces

2¼ cups (11½ oz/360 g) all-purpose flour

1 tsp baking soda

1 tsp salt

1 cup (8 oz/250 g) unsalted butter, at room temperature

⅔ cup (5 oz/155 g) granulated sugar

⅔ cup (5 oz/155 g) firmly packed light brown sugar

1 whole large egg, plus 1 egg yolk

2 Tbsp light corn syrup, honey, or maple syrup

2 tsp vanilla extract

12 oz (375 g) semisweet chocolate, chopped into ½-inch (12-mm) chunks

mix it up

Try pecans, almonds, or peanuts in place of the walnuts, and a mixture of semisweet, white chocolate, and milk chocolate chips. When using white chocolate or milk chocolate, use chips rather than chopped bar chocolate because chips hold their shape better when baked.

Preheat the oven to 350°F (180°C). Spread the walnuts in a single layer on a rimmed baking sheet. Place in the oven and toast, stirring occasionally, until fragrant and toasted, about 10 minutes. Let cool, then coarsely chop.

In a bowl, sift together the flour, baking soda, and salt. In another bowl, using an electric mixer on medium-high speed, beat together the butter and both sugars until the mixture is light in texture, about 3 minutes. Beat in the whole egg and egg yolk, then the corn syrup and vanilla. Reduce the speed to low and gradually add the flour mixture, beating just until smooth and stopping to scrape down the sides of the bowl as needed. Stir in the chocolate and walnuts, distributing them evenly throughout the dough. Cover and refrigerate until cold, at least 2 hours or up to 6 hours.

Position racks in the center and upper third of the oven and preheat to 350°F (180°C). Line 2 rimmed baking sheets with parchment paper.

Drop rounded tablespoonfuls of the chilled dough onto the baking sheets, spacing them about 1 inch (2.5 cm) apart. Place 1 sheet on each oven rack and bake, switching the pans between the racks and rotating them 180 degrees halfway through baking, until the cookies are lightly browned, 8–10 minutes. Let cool for 3 minutes on the baking sheets, then transfer to wire racks to cool slightly before serving.

Chewy Ginger-Molasses Cookies

Studded with hunks of crystallized ginger, these spicy cookies are crisp as well as chewy. They make great ice cream sandwiches: Simply squish a small scoop of softened vanilla ice cream between two cookies.

MAKES ABOUT 2½ DOZEN COOKIES

2 cups (10 oz/315 g) all-purpose flour

1½ tsp baking soda

½ tsp salt

1 tsp ground ginger

1 tsp ground cinnamon

¼ tsp ground allspice

¾ cup (6 oz/185 g) unsalted butter, at room temperature

1 cup (7 oz/220 g) firmly packed light brown sugar

1 large egg

½ cup (5½ oz/170 g) molasses

⅓–½ cup (2–3 oz/60–90 g) chopped crystallized ginger

Space 2 racks evenly in the oven and preheat to 350°F (180°C). Line 2 baking sheets with parchment paper.

In a bowl, sift together the flour, baking soda, salt, ginger, cinnamon, and allspice. In the bowl of a mixer fitted with the paddle attachment, beat the butter and sugar on medium-high speed until creamy. Add the egg and molasses and beat until smooth. Add the flour mixture and crystallized ginger and beat on low speed until incorporated.

Drop tablespoonfuls of the dough onto the prepared baking sheets, spacing the cookies well apart. Bake until the cookies are golden brown, about 12 minutes, rotating the pans about halfway through baking. Let the cookies cool on the pans for 5 minutes, then transfer to wire racks to cool completely.

baker's note

To make measuring thick, sticky molasses easier, lightly spray the measuring cup with cooking spray before pouring in the molasses. It will glide right out!

Millefeuille with Fresh Berries & Kiwi

This dessert takes its name from the French phrase mille feuille—*"one thousand leaves"—a slight exaggeration depicting its many layers of pastry. One-third of a standard frozen puff pastry sheet makes a single dessert that serves two. Triple the recipe for company.*

SERVES 2

1 frozen puff pastry sheet (about 8 oz/ 250 g), preferably all-butter

½ cup (4 oz/125 g) heavy cream

1½ tsp granulated sugar

3 kiwi fruits, peeled and thinly sliced

About ¾ cup (3 oz/90 g) mixed fresh blackberries and blueberries

Fresh mint sprigs for garnish

Confectioners' sugar for dusting

Preheat an oven to 400°F (200°C). Thaw the puff pastry sheet according to the package directions. Line a baking sheet with parchment paper.

Place the puff pastry sheet on a lightly floured work surface. Unfold the pastry and lay flat. Following the indentation from one of the folds, cut a strip of pastry about 3½ by 10 inches (9 by 25 cm), then cut crosswise into two even pieces. (Re-wrap and refreeze the remaining two-thirds of the pastry sheet to save for another use.) Place the pastry pieces on the prepared baking sheet. Using a fork, prick the pastry all over at even intervals to prevent over-puffing when baking.

Bake until just golden, about 15 minutes. Transfer to a rack and let cool.

Meanwhile, in a small bowl, combine the cream and granulated sugar. Beat with an electric mixer on medium-high speed until stiff peaks form, about 3 minutes.

Carefully split each piece of puffed pastry into two layers, making 4 layers in all. Place one layer on a plate. Spoon a third of the whipped cream over the pastry, then arrange half of the kiwi slices over the cream. Place a second layer of the pastry over the kiwis, spoon on another third of the cream, and half of the berries. Place a third layer of pastry over the berries, spoon on most of the remaining cream, and arrange the remaining kiwi slices over the cream. Top with the remaining pastry layer, the final spoonful of whipped cream, and the last of the berries. Dust the top with confectioners' sugar, garnish with mint sprigs, and serve.

This puff-pastry dessert is one of the easiest
and most delicious ways to showcase fresh
seasonal fruits. Fresh kiwis and berries make
a sublime combination for late summer,
but use any variety of fruit in season—from
strawberries and pineapple in spring to pears
and quince in fall.

love forever

There are never enough ways to express love.
Even the smallest thoughtful gesture—like this
heart-shaped tart—can make any day a special
occasion. Appreciate every moment together
and yours will be a happy partnership indeed.

Raspberry-Lemon Tart

When you and your sweetie want a special dessert, this is the one to try. If you don't have a heart-shaped pan, a 9-inch (23-cm) tart pan will do. Pair the tart with a few glasses of chilled sparkling wine or a pot of hot coffee to temper the sweetness.

SERVES 8

Tart Shell (page 250)

FOR THE LEMON CURD

3 large eggs

3 large egg yolks

½ cup (4 oz/125 g) sugar

¼ cup (½ oz/15 g) grated or minced lemon zest

½ cup (4 fl oz/125 ml) fresh lemon juice

¼ tsp salt

4 Tbsp (2 oz/60 g) butter, cubed and slightly softened

⅓ cup (3 oz/90 g) raspberry jam

½ tsp kirsch

2 cups (8 oz/250 g) fresh raspberries

Make the tart dough and bake as directed, using a 10-inch (25-cm) heart-shaped tart pan or a 9-inch (23-cm) round tart pan, each with a removable bottom. Let cool.

To make the lemon curd, in a nonreactive saucepan, whisk together the eggs, egg yolks, and sugar. Whisk in the lemon zest, lemon juice, and salt. Cook over low heat, whisking constantly, until the mixture turns bright yellow and is thick enough to coat the back of a wooden spoon, about 7 minutes. Do not boil. Remove the pan from the heat and whisk in the butter. Strain the mixture through a fine-mesh sieve into a clean bowl and nest the bowl in a larger bowl filled with ice water. Whisk occasionally until the lemon curd is completely cool. Transfer the curd to a smaller container, cover, and refrigerate until completely cold, about 2 hours.

To assemble the tart, in a small saucepan, combine the raspberry jam with the kirsch and stir over medium heat until warm and liquid, 3–4 minutes. To strain out the seeds, pour the jam mixture through a fine-mesh sieve held over a bowl, pressing against the mixture with the back of a spoon. Brush a very thin layer of the jam mixture over the bottom of the prebaked tart shell. Fill the shell with the chilled lemon curd and spread into an even layer, jiggling the shell gently so that the surface of the lemon curd is even. Place the raspberries on top of the curd in one snug layer, with the bottoms of the raspberries facing upward. Refrigerate the tart until ready to serve.

Kitchen Essentials

You probably received kitchenware as wedding gifts, and you most likely have collected some on your own, but now it's time to curate your kitchen arsenal so it works for the two of you. Start with the essential cookware that every kitchen needs, then add to it with ovenware and tools customized to suit your cooking styles and preferred techniques.

POTS & PANS

Don't worry about matching sets when it comes to cookware. Instead, quality should be your first consideration. The type of material and construction of your cookware can help you determine how it will cook and conduct heat, whether it will interact with certain foods, and how long it will last.

Here are the choices:

STAINLESS STEEL Long-lasting, durable, and easy to maintain, this is a top choice for cookware. Look for stainless-steel pots and pans clad with other materials, such as copper or aluminum, to help them heat up more quickly and evenly.

CAST IRON Heavy, durable, and classic, cast iron heats up slowly, holds heat well, and, with proper use, can be naturally nonstick. Enameled cast iron has been coated to prevent it from interacting with acidic foods; it goes from stove to oven beautifully.

NONSTICK For searing and frying with very little oil, today's nonstick coatings are eco-friendly, and nonstick surfaces are available for stainless-steel cookware and ceramic induction-top cookware as well.

COPPER The best conductor of heat, copper pots are used in many professional kitchens. The interior surface of most contemporary copper cookware is lined with stainless steel, making it durable, nonreactive, and easy to clean. Copper patinas with age; polish keeps it shiny.

ESSENTIAL POTS & PANS

Frying pans: one large cast iron and one medium nonstick

Saucepans: one small, one medium (with lids)

Sauté pan: one medium, one large (with lids)

Stockpot: one large (with lid)

Stove-top grill pan: one cast iron

OVENWARE

The hot, dry environment of the oven requires a few key pieces of equipment for roasting, baking, and braising. Serious bakers will likely need their own set of tools, geared specifically to the items they like to cook.

ESSENTIAL OVENWARE

Roasting pan (medium or large, with rack)

Enameled-iron Dutch oven (5–7 qt/4.75–6.5 l)

Rimless baking sheet

Rimmed baking sheet

Wire rack

Loaf pan (8½ by 4½ inches/21.5 by 11.5 cm)

Square baking dish (8 or 9 inch/20 or 23 cm)

Muffin pan (standard 12 cups)

Pie pan, glass (9 inch/23 cm)

Rectangular baking dish (9 by 13 inches/23 by 33 cm)

Tart pan with removable rim (9 or 10 inch/23 or 25 cm)

Two cake pans (8 or 9 inch/20 or 23 cm)

BAKEWARE

If there is a baker in the house, then no doubt he or she will want to curate their own collection of necessary tools. Since the cookware can vary according to individual recipes and methods of preparation, it can often be best to collect tools as you need them. The undeniable workhorse of nearly all bakers' kitchens, however, is a good-quality stand mixer with the standard attachments (whisk, paddle, and dough hook). With a stand mixer and some parchment paper or a silicone baking mat on hand, most baking recipes will be easier to manage.

Essential Tools

An old saying tells us, "There's a lid for every pot," meaning we all have a perfect mate out there. Now that you've found yours, update the saying to, "There's a tool for every task." You don't need every gadget ever made to do things efficiently, though. This list of kitchen tools will get you through a lifetime of great meals.

KNIVES

Along with your hands and a good pot, a sharp knife is undeniably in the trio of top culinary tools. Start with a chef's knife that feels comfortable in your hand, plus a sharp paring knife (if both of you are avid cooks, you may want two of each). The other essential knives are a serrated bread knife; a small serrated utility knife for tomatoes and other tough-skinned fruits and vegetables; and a slicing or carving knife for steaks, roasts, and poultry. If you hone knives on a sharpening steel (see below) or have them professionally sharpened on a regular basis, they can last decades.

Store knives on a magnetic wall strip or in a knife block—never loose in a drawer where the blades could get nicked and it could be dangerous for the person reaching into the drawer. Remember that a dull blade is more dangerous than a sharp one, so get in the habit of honing a knife every time you use it. Find a professional knife sharpener in your area and take in your knives whenever they start to feel dull. To safely transport them, you might want to invest in a knife carrying kit.

ESSENTIAL KNIVES

Chef's knife (8 or 11 inch/20 or 28 cm; one or two)

Paring knife

Serrated bread knife

Serrated small utility knife

Slicing/carving knife

Sharpening steel

HONING A KNIFE Routinely hone nonserrated knives whenever you use them to help maintain the edges between professional sharpenings. Hold the knife blade at about a 15-degree angle to the sharpening steel and swipe in an arc from top to bottom along the length of the steel three or four times per blade side.

COOKING TOOLS

Among the first tools you likely added to your kitchen were the basic electrics—blender, food processor, stand and/or handheld mixer, toaster—that most cooks use on a regular basis. Beyond those small appliances is a long list of basic tools that will see you through the preparation of most recipes. Although many are popular as wedding gifts, there may be a few you still need to purchase.

ESSENTIAL TOOLS

Basting brushes

Box grater

Bulb baster

Can opener and corkscrew

Citrus reamer or press

Colander and sieve

Cutting boards: wooden or plastic

Garlic press

Instant-read thermometer

Kitchen shears

Measuring spoons

Microplane zester

Mixing bowls: stainless steel (small and large)

Nested metal measuring cups

Glass measuring pitchers

Pastry scraper

Pepper grinder

Potato masher

Salad spinner

Spatulas: metal and silicone

Spoons: slotted, solid, and wooden

Steamer basket

Tongs

Vegetable peeler

Pot holders & lots of kitchen towels

Chicken Stock

5 lb (2.5 kg) chicken backs and necks
1 yellow onion, quartered
2 carrots, peeled and cut in half
1 rib celery, cut in half
2 sprigs fresh parsley
1 sprig fresh thyme
½ bay leaf
1 tsp salt (optional)

In a large stockpot, combine the chicken parts with 4 quarts (4 l) water and bring to a boil over high heat. Reduce the heat to low and use a large spoon to skim off any gray foam that rises to the surface. (Do not skim off the fat as it retains much of the flavor.) Add the onion, carrots, celery, parsley, thyme, bay leaf, and salt (if using). Reduce the heat to low and simmer gently, uncovered, until the stock tastes rich and is a light golden color, about 3 hours. Strain the stock through a fine-mesh sieve and let cool. Using the spoon, skim off any fat from the surface. Use immediately or cover and refrigerate for up to 3 days (remove the hardened white fat from the surface after chilling), or freeze for up to 2 months.

MAKES ABOUT 3 QUARTS (3 L)

Beef Stock

6 lb (3 kg) meaty beef shanks and knuckles
3 carrots, cut into 2-inch (5-cm) pieces
2 yellow onions, quartered
3 ribs celery, cut into 2-inch (5-cm) pieces
4 sprigs fresh parsley
2 sprigs fresh thyme
½ bay leaf
5 peppercorns
1 tsp salt (optional)

Preheat the oven to 425°F (220°C). Arrange the beef shanks and knuckles in a single layer in a heavy roasting pan and roast, turning once, until thoroughly browned, 20–25 minutes. In a large stockpot, combine the roasted bones with 5 quarts(5 l) water and bring to a boil over high heat. Meanwhile, place the roasting pan with the drippings over 2 burners and turn the heat to medium-high. Add ⅓ cup (3 fl oz/ 80 ml) water to the roasting pan and bring to a brisk simmer. Deglaze the pan, stirring and scraping with a wooden spatula to loosen the browned bits from the pan bottom. Add the flavorful pan drippings to the pot. When the stock reaches a boil, use a large metal spoon to skim off any gray foam that rises to the surface. Add the carrots, onions, celery, parsley, thyme, bay leaf, peppercorns, and salt, if using. Reduce the heat to low and simmer gently until the stock tastes rich and is a light caramel color, about 5 hours. Strain the stock through a fine-mesh sieve and let cool.

Skim off any fat that has risen to the surface and refrigerate. Season to taste before using. Use immediately or cover and refrigerate for up to 3 days, or freeze for up to 2 months

MAKES ABOUT 3 QUARTS (3 L)

Vegetable Stock

2 yellow onions, thickly sliced
1 leek, well rinsed and thickly sliced
2 carrots, peeled and coarsely chopped
2 ribs celery, coarsely chopped
3 or 4 sprigs fresh parsley
6 black peppercorns
1 bay leaf
2 sprigs fresh thyme

In a large stockpot, combine all the ingredients with 4 quarts (4 l) water and bring to a boil over high heat. Reduce the heat to low and simmer gently, uncovered, for 1 hour. Strain the stock through a fine-mesh sieve, pressing on the vegetables with the back of a spoon to extract as much liquid as possible. Discard the vegetables. Use immediately or cover and refrigerate for up to 3 days, or freeze for up to 2 months.

MAKES ABOUT 3½ QUARTS (3½ L)

Basil Pesto

1 or 2 cloves garlic
¼ cup (1 oz/40 g) pine nuts
2 cups (2 oz/60 g) packed fresh basil leaves
½ cup (4 fl oz/125 ml) extra-virgin olive oil
½ cup (2 oz/60 g) freshly grated Parmesan cheese
Salt and freshly ground pepper

With a food processor running, drop the garlic through the feed tube and process until minced. Turn off the processor, add the pine nuts, and pulse a few times to chop. Add the basil and pulse a few times to chop coarsely. Then, with the processor running, add the oil through the feed tube in a slow, steady stream and process until a smooth, moderately thick paste forms, stopping to scrape down the bowl as needed. Transfer to a bowl and stir in the Parmesan. Season to taste with salt and pepper. Use the pesto at once, or transfer to a storage container, top with a thin layer of oil, cover, and refrigerate for up to 1 week.

MAKES ABOUT 1 CUP (8 OZ/250 G)

KALE PESTO Replace the basil with stemmed kale. Replace the pine nuts with almonds.

ARUGULA PESTO Replace the basil with arugula, or use 1 part arugula and 1 part fresh mint leaves.

CILANTRO PESTO Replace the basil with fresh cilantro and add 1 teaspoon grated lemon zest.

Perfect Hard-Boiled Eggs

3 or 4 fresh large eggs
Salt

Prepare an ice bath by putting 2–3 cups (16–24 fl oz/ 500–750 ml) water and ice in a large bowl.

In a saucepan, bring 1 quart (1 l) salted water to a full boil over high heat. Lower the eggs gently into the water with a slotted spoon and reduce the heat to medium-low to maintain a gentle simmer (and prevent eggs from cracking against the pot). Exactly 8 minutes after adding the eggs to the water, remove them with the slotted spoon and plunge them into the ice bath to stop the cooking. When cool, crack and peel the eggs.

Torn Croutons

¼ lb (125 g) day-old country-style sourdough bread, crusts removed
3 Tbsp unsalted butter, melted
Salt and freshly ground pepper

Preheat the oven to 400°F (200°C). Tear the bread into ½-inch (12-mm) pieces and place on a baking sheet. Drizzle the butter over the bread, sprinkle with salt and pepper, and toss to coat. Bake until golden and crisp, 10–15 minutes. Let cool.

MAKES ABOUT 1 CUP (1½ OZ/45 G)

Dijon Vinaigrette

1 Tbsp white wine vinegar or red wine vinegar
1 tsp finely chopped shallot
½ tsp Dijon mustard
3–4 Tbsp extra-virgin olive oil
Salt and freshly ground pepper

In a jar, combine the vinegar, shallot, mustard, olive oil, and salt and pepper to taste. Cover and shake until well blended.

MAKES ABOUT ¼ CUP (2 FL OZ/60 ML)

Mayonnaise

1 large egg
1 tsp Dijon mustard
1 tsp lemon juice or white wine vinegar
1 tsp salt
¼ tsp freshly ground pepper
¾ cup (6 fl oz/180 ml) vegetable oil
¾ cup (6 fl oz/180 ml) extra-virgin olive oil

Warm the uncracked egg in a bowl of hot tap water for 3 minutes. In a blender or food processor, combine the egg, mustard, lemon juice, salt, and pepper. In a bowl, combine the oils. With the motor running, slowly drizzle the oils into the blender (this should take several minutes) to make a thick mayonnaise. Stir in 1 tablespoon hot water.

MAKES 1¾ CUPS (14 FL OZ/430 ML)

Simple Béarnaise Sauce

6 large egg yolks
1 cup (8 oz/250 g) unsalted butter
Juice of 1 lemon
⅛ tsp cayenne pepper
Salt
1 Tbsp chopped fresh tarragon
½ tsp tarragon vinegar or white wine vinegar
3 Tbsp hot water

In a blender, process the egg yolks until creamy and pale yellow. In a small saucepan over low heat, melt the butter, adding the lemon juice and cayenne before the butter solids separate from the liquid. Increase the heat to medium and bring to a boil. Remove from the heat and pour into a small pitcher. With the blender running at medium speed, slowly pour the hot butter mixture into the egg yolks and process until smooth. Season with ½ teaspoon salt. In the pitcher, mix together the tarragon, vinegar, and hot water and pour enough of the mixture into the sauce to achieve a good consistency. Serve right away, or pour into a thermos, cover, and set aside for up to 4 hours.

MAKES 1½ CUPS (12 FL OZ/275 ML)

Harissa

3 oz (90 g) dried New Mexico or other large dried red chiles (12–14)
2 roasted red bell peppers, stemmed and seeded, or ½ cup (3 oz/90 g) drained bottled roasted red peppers
3 Tbsp olive oil, plus more for storing
2 Tbsp fresh lemon juice
4 cloves garlic
½ tsp fine sea salt
¼ tsp ground coriander
¼ tsp ground cumin

Put the chiles in a heatproof bowl and cover with boiling water. Let stand until softened, about 30 minutes. Drain and remove the stems, leaving some soaking liquid inside most of the chiles. Place the chiles in the bowl of a food processor. Add the roasted red peppers, 3 tablespoons olive oil, the lemon juice, garlic, salt, coriander, and cumin. Process, stopping to scrape down the sides of the bowl 2 or 3 times, until the mixture forms a paste. Taste and adjust the seasoning. To store, pour the sauce into a glass jar with a tight-fitting lid, cover the surface of the sauce with olive oil, and store in the refrigerator for up to 2 weeks.

MAKES ABOUT 1½ CUPS (12 FL OZ/275 ML)

Chipotle Spice Paste

¼ cup (2 fl oz/60 ml) olive oil
1 cup (1 oz/30 g) loosely packed fresh cilantro
4 cloves garlic, coarsely chopped
3 chipotle chiles in adobo sauce, chopped
2 Tbsp ground cumin
2 Tbsp ground coriander
1 Tbsp dry mustard
Salt and freshly ground pepper
Fresh lime juice

In a blender or food processor, combine the oil, cilantro, garlic, chipotle chiles, cumin, coriander, mustard, 1 tablespoon salt, and 2 tablespoons pepper. Pulse to chop roughly, then process until smooth. Season to taste with lime juice. Use right away, or cover and refrigerate for up to 1 week.

MAKES ABOUT 1 CUP (8 OZ/250 G)

Chipotle Spice Rub

2 tsp chipotle chile powder
2 tsp brown sugar
1 tsp paprika
1 tsp dry mustard powder
1 tsp ground cumin
1 tsp salt

In a jar with a lid, combine the chipotle powder, sugar, paprika, mustard powder, cumin, and salt. Cover and shake until well mixed.

MAKES ABOUT 2½ TABLESPOONS

Herb-Spice Rub

2 cloves garlic, minced
1 Tbsp minced fresh sage leaves
1 Tbsp minced fresh thyme leaves
1 tsp minced fresh rosemary
1 tsp ground coriander
½ tsp paprika
½ tsp ground allspice
½ tsp fresh lemon zest

In a small bowl, combine the garlic, sage, thyme, rosemary, coriander, paprika, allspice, and lemon zest. Stir to blend.

MAKES ABOUT ¼ CUP (¾ OZ/20 G)

Ultra Chocolate Doughnut Glaze

2 cups (8 oz/250 g) confectioners' sugar
¼ lb (4 oz/125 g) semisweet chocolate
5 Tbsp (2½ oz/75 g) butter
1½ tsp vanilla extract
¼ tsp salt

In a bowl, combine ¼ cup (2 fl oz/60 ml) hot water with the sugar, chocolate, butter, vanilla, and salt and stir to combine. Place the bowl over simmering water in a pan set over medium heat and cook, stirring occasionally, until the chocolate is melted and the mixture is smooth, 2–3 minutes.

MAKES ENOUGH FOR 1 DOZEN 3-INCH (7.5-CM) DOUGHNUTS

Salted Caramel Doughnut Glaze

1½ cups (12 oz/375 g) sugar
1 tsp fresh lemon juice
1½ cups (12 fl oz/375 ml) heavy cream
1½ tsp flaky sea salt, plus more for sprinkling

In a saucepan, combine the sugar and lemon juice. Add ¼ cup (2 fl oz/60 ml) water and place over medium heat. Cook, stirring continuously, until the mixture bubbles vigorously and turns a golden amber color, 7–9 minutes. Remove from the heat and immediately and very carefully add the cream (the mixture will bubble and splatter). Stir until the sauce is smooth, then stir in the salt. After glazing, sprinkle more salt evenly over each doughnut top.

MAKES ENOUGH FOR 1 DOZEN 3-INCH (7.5-CM) DOUGHNUTS

Meyer Lemon Doughnut Glaze with Pistachios

2½ cups (10 oz/315 g) confectioners' sugar
6 Tbsp (3 oz/90 g) butter, melted
2 Tbsp fresh Meyer lemon juice
½ cup (2 oz/60 g) chopped pistachios

In a bowl, combine the sugar, butter, and lemon juice with 3 tablespoons hot water and whisk until smooth. Whisk in more hot water, 1 teaspoon at a time, if needed. After glazing, sprinkle the pistachios evenly over each doughnut top.

MAKES ENOUGH FOR 16 3-INCH (7.5-CM) DOUGHNUTS

Double-Crust Flaky Pie Dough

2 cups (10 oz/315 g) all-purpose flour

½ tsp salt

1 tsp sugar (optional; omit if making a savory dish)

¾ cup (6 oz/185 g) very cold unsalted butter, cut into cubes

8 Tbsp (4 fl oz/125 ml) ice water, plus more if needed

In the bowl of a food processor, mix the flour, salt, and sugar, if using. Sprinkle the butter over the top and pulse for a few seconds, or just until the butter is slightly broken up into the flour but still in visible pieces. Evenly sprinkle the water over the flour mixture, then process just until the mixture starts to come together. Dump the dough onto a work surface, press it together, then divide it in half. Press each half into a disk and wrap in plastic wrap. Refrigerate the dough for 30 minutes or up to 1 day, or freeze for up to 1 month.

MAKES ENOUGH FOR ONE 9-INCH (23-CM) DOUBLE-CRUST PIE OR SIX 5-INCH (13-CM) MINI PIES

Single-Crust Flaky Pie Dough

1¼ cups (6½ oz/200 g) all-purpose flour

¼ tsp salt

½ tsp sugar (optional; omit if making a savory dish)

17 Tbsp (3½ oz/105 g) very cold unsalted butter, cut into cubes

5 Tbsp (3 fl oz/80 ml) ice water, plus more if needed

In the bowl of a food processor, mix the flour, salt, and sugar, if using. Sprinkle the butter over the top and pulse for a few seconds, or just until the butter is slightly broken up into the flour but still in visible pieces. Evenly sprinkle the water over the flour mixture, then process just until the mixture starts to come together. Dump the dough into a large lock-top plastic bag, and press into a flat disk. Refrigerate the dough for 30 minutes or up to 1 day, or freeze for up to 1 month.

MAKES ENOUGH FOR ONE 9-INCH (23-CM) SINGLE-CRUST PIE OR TART

Tart Shell

1 cup (5 oz/155 g) all-purpose flour

1 Tbsp sugar

½ tsp salt

½ cup (4 oz/125 g) cold butter, cut into ½-inch (12-mm) pieces

½ tsp vanilla extract

In a bowl, stir together the flour, sugar, and salt. Work the butter into the flour mixture with your fingertips, pressing and blending until the butter looks granular and the mixture begins to hold together. In a small cup or bowl, combine 1 tablespoon water and the vanilla. Drizzle the vanilla mixture over the flour mixture and mix with a fork until the ingredients are well combined and the pastry holds together when pressed. Gather the dough into a ball and wrap it in plastic wrap.

Let the dough rest for 30 minutes to allow the flour to absorb the moisture. Then, use your fingertips to press the pastry into the bottom and sides of a 9-inch (23-cm) round or 10-inch (25-cm) heart-shaped tart pan, making sure it is distributed evenly. Cover and place the tart shell in the freezer for 30 minutes to firm.

Preheat the oven to 375°F (190°C). Remove the tart shell from the freezer and bake until light golden brown, 20–25 minutes. Let cool before filling.

MAKES ENOUGH FOR ONE ROUND 9-INCH (23-CM) TART OR ONE HEART-SHAPED 10-INCH (25-CM) TART

Pizza Dough

1 envelope (2¼ tsp) active dry yeast

¼ cup (2 fl oz/60 ml) warm water (105°–115°F/40°–46°C)

¼ cup (2 fl oz/60 ml) extra-virgin olive oil, plus more for greasing

1½ tsp salt

1 tsp sugar

3 cups (15 oz/470 g) bread flour, plus more for dusting

Cornmeal for dusting

At least 10 hours before making pizza or calzone, in a small bowl, sprinkle the yeast over the warm water and let stand until foamy, about 5 minutes. Transfer the yeast mixture to the bowl of a stand mixer fitted with the paddle attachment. Add 1 cup (8 fl oz/250 ml) cold water, the oil, salt, and sugar. With the mixer on medium-low speed, add enough flour to make a soft dough that does not stick to the sides of the bowl. Stop the machine and cover the bowl with a kitchen towel, wrapping it around the paddle attachment. Let stand for 10 minutes.

Remove the towel and the paddle attachment and fit the mixer with the dough hook attachment. Knead the dough on medium speed, stopping the machine and pulling the dough off the hook if it climbs up, until the dough is smooth and supple, about 8 minutes. Transfer the dough to a lightly floured work surface and knead by hand for 1 minute. Shape the dough into a taut ball.

Lightly oil a large bowl. Add the dough, turn to coat with the oil, and place smooth side up. Cover the bowl tightly with plastic wrap. Refrigerate until doubled, at least 8 or up to 36 hours. Remove the dough from the refrigerator 1 to 2 hours before shaping.

MAKES ENOUGH FOR TWO 12-INCH (33-CM) PIZZAS

Index

weldon**owen**

1045 Sansome Street, Suite 100
San Francisco, CA 94111
www.weldonowen.com

Weldon Owen is a division of Bonnier Publishing USA

Weldon Owen, Inc.
President & Publisher Roger Shaw
SVP, Sales & Marketing Amy Kaneko
Finance & Operations Director Philip Paulick

Associate Publisher Amy Marr
Senior Editor Lisa Atwood

Creative Director Kelly Booth
Art Director Alexandra Zeigler
Senior Production Designer Rachel Lopez Metzger

Production Director Chris Hemesath
Associate Production Director Michelle Duggan

Imaging Manager Don Hill

Photographer John Kernick
Digital Tech/Photographer's Assistant Rizwan A. Alvi
Food Stylist Alison Attenborough
Food Stylist Assistants Alex Leonard,
Brett Regot, Karolina Wojcik
Prop Stylists Alistair Turnbull, Maya Rossi
Prop Stylists Assistants Kelsie Conley, Kate Donovan,
Layla Kenney, John Lingenfelter

Newlywed Cookbook
Conceived and produced by Weldon Owen, Inc.
In collaboration with Williams Sonoma, Inc.
3250 Van Ness Avenue, San Francisco, CA 94109

A Weldon Owen Production
Copyright © 2016 Weldon Owen Inc.
and Williams Sonoma, Inc.

Printed and bound in China by 1010 International

First printed in 2016
10 9 8 7 6 5 4 3 2

Library of Congress Cataloging-in-Publication
data is available.

ISBN 13: 978-1-68188-141-6
ISBN 10: 1-68188-141-1

Acknowledgments
Weldon Owen wishes to thank the following people
for their generous support in producing this book:
Lesley Bruynesteyn, Pranavi Chopra, Kate Chynoweth, Peggy Fallon,
Gloria Geller, Denise Griffiths, Dana Jacobi, Eve Lynch,
Alexis Mersel, Carolyn Miller, Elizabeth Parson, Tori Ritchie,
Sharon Silva, Emely Vertiz, and Tamara White.

Photography Credits
All photographs by John Kernick except:
Ali Harper, pages 4 and 130; Getty Images, page 8;
iStock, page 16; Stocksy, page 26 and 111;
Anais & Dax/AUGUST, page 54; Masterfile, page 201.